And the Life of the World to Come

And the Life of the World to Come

Reflections on Biblical Notions of Heaven

John F. Craghan

LITURGICAL PRESS

Collegeville, Minnesota

www.litpress.org

Cover design by Ann Blattner. Photo: Hemera/Thinkstock.

Nihil Obstat: Reverend Robert Harren, *Censor deputatus.*
Imprimatur: ✠ Most Reverend John F. Kinney, J.C.D., D.D., Bishop of Saint Cloud, Minnesota, April 2, 2012.

1   2   3   4   5   6   7   8   9

Library of Congress Cataloging-in-Publication Data

Craghan, John F.
    And the life of the world to come : reflections on biblical notions of
heaven / John F. Craghan.
        p. cm.
    ISBN 978-0-8146-3413-4 — ISBN 978-0-8146-3414-1
    1. Heaven—Biblical teaching.   2. Future life—Biblical teaching.   I. Title.
BS680.H42C734   2012
236'.24—dc23   2011051513

In

grateful and loving memory

of

my parents, Margaret and John Craghan,

who

taught me that heaven means being *with*

Contents

Preface

One may legitimately inquire why I am so preoccupied with heaven. To begin with, I am already a septuagenarian. I have witnessed not only the passing of my parents but also that of many peers. In reading the daily newspaper, I seem to spend an inordinate amount of time with the obituaries. I keep asking myself when my name will appear in that section and what the piece will actually say. Each year my list of Mass intentions grows longer and longer. I also wonder whether someone will have a Mass said for me after my death. My body tells me that I am no longer the dashing athlete of former days. I constantly hear my father's perceptive remark, "John, as you grow older, all you will get are flats and blowouts." My father also used to sing this song that makes a greater impression on me with each passing day: "I used to be the life of the party forty-five years ago but I can't do the things I used to do forty-five years ago."

Given this situation, I naturally inquire about heaven. I want to know what it is like and who will be there. At the same time I am anxious to know what I will look like and how I will remain connected to my loved ones still on earth. I am also eager to discover how heaven relates to my liturgical life—specifically about the link between baptism and Eucharist, on the one hand, and my heavenly existence, on the other. At this point I find myself with more questions than answers.

To console myself, I observe that these questions radically differ from some popular conceptions of heaven, at least for those who accept some belief in an afterlife. Examples of such conceptions include the following. Heaven means only geographical confinement in a casket where one passes the time pushing up daisies. Heaven is nothing other than a cold-water flat in contradistinction to hell that is steam heat and hot water. Heaven is a place of sorts where one parades about in white gowns supported by angel-like wings. The inhabitants of heaven, therefore, must learn to navigate those clouds in order to avoid falling. Obviously a course like Celestial Navigation 101 is obligatory. As for musical instruments, the harp is the instrument of choice. Regarding the issue of geography, heaven is "way up there" as opposed to our usual terra firma. The entrance to this residence is the pearly gates where one must pass muster with St. Peter. In the final analysis, heaven is a place of bliss exempt from health problems, taxes, and the empty promises of politicians who are always long on talk and short on production. The following quote seems to capture the peacefulness of the heavenly realm: "I thought I died and went to heaven."

Not satisfied with these and similar observations, I have decided to turn to the Bible in an attempt to mine its treasures and ferret out its wealth of traditions. I begin with the Old Testament in its ancient Near Eastern setting, trying to discover what death really means to our biblical ancestors. Admittedly I focus more on the New Testament for reasons that will soon become obvious. I do not follow a strict chronological order, for example, beginning with the first writing (1 Thessalonians) and concluding with the last (probably 2 Peter). Instead, I first examine the Synoptic Gospels (Matthew, Mark, and Luke) and Acts. I start with Mark since both Matthew and Luke use that gospel for their own compositions. I then consider the Fourth Gospel followed by the Pauline traditions. This phrase includes the genuine letters of Paul as well as those attributed to him. (Here I attempt to follow a probable chronological order for such letters.) After the Pauline traditions, I consider Hebrews and conclude with Revelation/Apocalypse.

At the outset I must forewarn the reader that I focus on heaven, not purgatory, hell, or the particular and universal judgments. However, the study of heaven necessarily includes the notion of the resurrection of the body, even though the New Testament does not discuss their mutual relationship. I seek not only to interpret the biblical passages but also to reflect on them. Hence this work is not a dry exercise in the literature of the ancient Near East. Instead, it intends to address certain contemporary problems and issues. I thus hope to challenge the reader to see and understand heaven from the perspective of the biblical authors as they relate to our questions and anxieties. I therefore wholeheartedly encourage the reader to have Bible in hand in order to consult the appropriate texts. There is no substitute for knowing what the text actually says. To this end, I have provided the key biblical passages at the beginning of each chapter.

Finally, a word about the title. "And the life of the world to come" follows upon "the resurrection of the body" in the Nicene Creed that Catholics recite every Sunday at Mass. I often wonder what goes through the worshipers' minds when they profess this particular article of the creed. Are they focusing on heaven as a given geographical place somewhere in the universe or are they concentrating on the company or community that occupies this space? Are they perhaps thinking of the Trinity and their association with the Father, the Son, and the Holy Spirit? No doubt other thoughts pass through their minds as they acknowledge in faith life after death. I trust that the examination and reflection on the pertinent biblical texts will provide some answers to these questions. Since the afterlife remains somewhat confusing for not a few believers, the time devoted to this inquiry appears well justified.

Finally I wish to thank my wife Barbara Lynne for her attentive reading of the whole manuscript and for her many helpful suggestions. Such care also attests to the being *with* dimension of heaven.

Easter 2011

John F. Craghan

CHAPTER ONE

The Old Testament in Its Ancient Near Eastern Setting

Key Biblical Passages: Genesis 5:21-24; 37:20-35; 48:8-11; 1 Samuel 2:1-10; 2 Kings 2:9-12; Psalms 16; 36; 46; 88; 104:1-9; Isaiah 38:10-20; Jonah 2:3-10

To appreciate the Bible's notions of an afterlife, it is useful to consider the influences that emanated from its neighbors, specifically Mesopotamia (the land between the Tigris and Euphrates Rivers—roughly modern Iraq) and Canaan (roughly the eastern Mediterranean). Since ancient Israel did not live in splendid isolation, it was exposed to the traditions and theologies of these regions, some of which have clearly impacted the Bible. To know something about such legacies is ultimately to appreciate the development of Israel's relationship with God.

Mesopotamia

In ancient Mesopotamia there are no beliefs in any of the following: a new age commencing at the end of the world, a resurrection of the body, a last judgment, a heaven or hell. After proper mourning rites and burial, one begins the journey to the netherworld. Offerings and gifts play a significant role in placating the netherworld gods who thus provide a proper welcome upon arrival. The journey involves considerable hazards such as a demon-controlled steppe and a dangerous river. Quite appropriately the abode of the dead is named "the land of no return." The dead live only a shadowy form of existence, a rather bleak imitation of their former life. Their surroundings are gloomy, although some texts speak of ghosts or spirits eating bread and drinking water. In this world they come under the strict supervision of a type of state structure. The proper authorities welcome each new arrival, instruct him or her about the netherworld's regulations, and assign the person his or her place. Vices or virtues count for nothing.

The happiness of the occupants of the netherworld depends on the quality and quantity of the funerary offerings that the living, especially the nuclear family, have to provide. As long as these offerings continue, the ghosts or spirits remain more or less peaceful. However, vengeful ghosts or spirits, for example, those who die a violent death, have to be controlled by expulsion rites.

Dying introduces a gradual weakening of the bonds between the deceased and the living. After several generations, the dead are reduced to ancestral spirits. Ancient Mesopotamians accept such beliefs as a matter of course since death is a fact of life. Even the great heroes such as Gilgamesh, the Beowulf of the ancient Near East, have to expect death. According to their theology, when the gods create humans, they determine death for them but retain life in their own hands.

Canaan

At the moment of death the Canaanites believe that everyone encounters the god Mot, the divine personification of death, and follows him into the netherworld. The deceased survive in a kind of subterranean afterlife that is the abode of the divine Mot. Here there is no question of judgment. A rather unpleasant but equal fate awaits all the dead who have first to pass through two mountains or under that area to get to the barren land of the dead that resembles a stronghold.

There is a certain solidarity between the living and the dead. As in Mesopotamia, the living have to provide the offerings and necessities that are impossible to get in the netherworld. Hence it is absolutely important to have descendants who care for their parents not only in life but also in death. A cult of the dead is a prescribed ritual, a type of wake that involves heavy drinking in an effort to make contact with the dead. For the Canaanites death does not prevent a type of ongoing community between the deceased and their survivors.

As in Mesopotamia, immortality remains a prerogative of the gods. When the goddess Anat promises the mortal Aqhat absolute immortality in exchange for his bow, the youth cannot be fooled. He boldly announces to the goddess that he will die the death of everyman. There are no exceptions to death's inflexible hold on humans.

Death in the Old Testament

In the Old Testament "death" can be employed in at least three ways. First, death functions as a metaphor for everything that constricts living life to the fullest, for example, deep depression, anxiety, illness, persecution, and the like. In Deuteronomy 30:15 Moses challenges his people to decide for or against their God in these terms: "See, I have today set before you life and good, death and evil." Second, death appears as a power that resists the divine order of creation. In Job 18:12-13 Bildad describes the fate of the wicked in this way: "His strength is famished, / disaster is ready at his side, / His skin is eaten to the limbs, / the firstborn of Death eats his limbs." Third, death is humankind's liminal experience of biological cessation. In the biblical view the entire human person enjoys a life force or energy conferred by the Creator (Gen 2:7: breath; Gen 6:3: spirit). At death this life force or energy returns to God (Eccl 12:7). In this condition one is only a shadowy remnant of one's former self and is usually called a "shade" (e.g., Ps 88:11).

In the first and third senses death is the opposite of life. Life represents the opportunity to be oneself to the fullest extent, including freedom, happiness, joy, communion with others, and so forth. Such a manner of living confirms the adage that life is worth living. Death, on the other hand, is much more than the absence of physical life. Whenever one experiences calamity, serious depression, harassment, and the like, one is dead. Whether death functions as a metaphor or as the termination of the vital functions, one must deal with Sheol.

Sheol

Sheol (the netherworld) is a subterranean region since the Bible consistently speaks of "going down." It is also the lowest place imaginable. To speak of Sheol is to conjure up a murky, miry area replete with dangerous seas, treacherous marshes, and chaotic waters (see Jonah 2:3-6). It is also described as a city with gates and bars that appear to discourage any form of escape. Darkness, dust, and silence also characterize this abode.

Sheol is also depicted as a monster of sorts that devours its victims (Num 16:32). It possesses an insatiable appetite: "Therefore Sheol enlarges its throat / and opens its mouth beyond measure" (Isa 5:14). Such an appetite recalls the voracious maw of the god Mot of the Canaanite netherworld. The use of the metaphor "pit" suggests a much reduced, weary form of existence. This gloomy view of the ultimate human destiny reflects the Mesopotamian and Canaanite influences. Although the Bible clearly prohibits communication with the dead (Lev 19:31; 20:27), a passage such as Deuteronomy 26:13 ("I have purged my house of the sacred portion" [the tithe on one's portion given to the dead]) suggests otherwise.

Who Goes to Sheol?

According to the conventional view both the righteous and the wicked inhabit this gloomy subterranean region. As Ecclesiastes 9:2 puts it, "Everything is the same for everybody: the same lot for the just and the wicked, for the good, for the clean and the unclean." According to this outlook God does not distinguish between saint and sinner. However, Psalm 16:10 confidently asserts that God will not permit his faithful ones to see the pit/Sheol. To summarize, the Old Testament appears to support two different theologies regarding the fate of the dead.

One should observe that the Bible mentions Sheol whenever death occurs owing to unnatural causes. On the other hand, whenever death takes place in its natural course, Sheol is not mentioned. Death in its natural course embraces the experience of divine blessing when a person sleeps or lies with one's fathers or kin. This non-Sheol vision of death goes hand in hand with the continuation of one's blood line, especially through numerous progeny. Thus Job dies when he is old and full of days in the company of his great-grandchildren (Job 42:16-17). So also the patriarch Jacob dies as the recipient of divine blessing since he sees his son Joseph and his children (Gen 48:11). This scene contrasts sharply with the one in which Jacob first receives word of Joseph's apparent death: "I will go down mourning to my son in Sheol" (Gen 37:35).

A "bad" death, namely, one linked to Sheol, can take several forms. It can be premature by occurring before one attains one's full potential. When King Hezekiah learns of his imminent death at an early age, he laments, "In the noontime of life I said, / I must depart! / To the gates of Sheol I have been consigned / for the rest of my years" (Isa 38:10). It can be violent, especially involving bloodshed, for example, Samuel's prediction of Saul's death at the hands of the Philistines (1 Sam 28:19-20). It can also be a death without a surviving heir (see Abram's reply to God in Gen 15:2-3).

Sheol is not reducible to a form of hell. One may think of it as the perpetuation of the decedent's unfulfilled life (especially a violent end). On the other hand, death linked to divine favor (the continuation of one's lineage, etc.) does not correspond to the later Judeo-Christian notion of heaven. Rather, this form of death concerns itself with fulfillment. Death in the form of divine favor does not imply a move to a "higher" place. In addition to the continuation of one's extended family, this death is associated with the memory of the deceased. According to Proverbs 10:7, "The memory of the just serves as blessing." One thus survives, not only in descendants, but also in one's name. This is the precise opposite of "I'll never forget what's his name."

This whole discussion reflects the central role of community. There is a survival of sorts whenever one's lineage continues and one's name is remembered. In this context the deceased retain their identity and thus do not constitute a multitude of nameless, forgotten individuals. Hence they remain members of the community. This community link will become an important building block in the development of the notion of heaven. The concept of fulfillment also plays a significant role in this evolution. At the same time it raises for the twenty-first century the question of genuine fulfillment. Is fulfillment merely the amassing of wealth and power? Is fulfillment synonymous with making it to the top? These are questions that the Bible will not only consider but also extend as a challenge.

Heaven

In the Old Testament, as well as in the New Testament, heaven means, in the first place, the sky above that is thought to be a dome. It functions as a firmament that holds back a mass of water. It also serves as a tent that protects humans living on earth (Ps 104:2). The expression "heaven and earth" encapsulates the entire created universe, suggesting a significant relationship between both areas. However, heaven also functions as God's dwelling place, implying a certain dimension of inaccessibility (Ps 150:1). Biblical authors depict God as enthroned above heaven. He is wrapped in light, clothed in majesty, and rides on the wings of the wind (Ps 104:1-3). Such images capture God's exalted state in heaven as creator and ruler. It is not surprising, therefore, that King Cyrus of Persia speaks of the God of Israel as "[t]he LORD, the God of heaven" (2 Chr 36:23).

Is this God of heaven totally remote from the lives of ordinary humans? In other words, is there some form of contact between the heavenly and the earthly, so that one may legitimately pray "Our Father, who art in heaven"? The Jerusalem temple offers a positive answer to such queries. It is Eden regained, a paradise that offers hope to those who seek God there. Such a God is the fountain of life (Ps 36:10). According to Psalm 133:3 the dew of Mount Hermon falls on the mountains of Zion, providing a liberation of sorts from the inroads of time that tend to erode ordinary human life. To journey to the temple is to reconnect with Israel's life-giving God of heaven who yet dwells among his people: "God is in its midst. . . . The LORD of hosts is with us; our stronghold is the God of Jacob" (Ps 46:6, 8).

Intimations of Surviving Death

Prior to the second century BC there is no indisputable biblical evidence for the notion of eternal life. However, in both the Bible and the world of religious experience the metaphor of rising or being raised from the dead implies at least the aspiration of somehow overcoming death. In biblical tradition this human hope springs from belief in a God who is thought to be the source of all life. In her song Hannah expresses this outlook in these words: "The LORD puts to death and gives life, casts down to Sheol and brings up again" (1 Sam 2:6). In addition to the metaphor of rising/being raised the Bible also contains passages related to the desire for the abiding enjoyment of God's presence. The psalms, in particular, speak of this ongoing communion with the God of Israel (see Pss 36:10; 56:14; 116:8-9). To repeat, all such passages at best intimate this strong desire and hope for a meaningful life after death. Only in the second century BC do such desires and hopes come to a clear, unequivocal expression.

Enoch (the antediluvian who walked with God) and Elijah (the ninth-century Israelite prophet) are two figures whose earthly lives come to an end without the experience of death. According to Genesis 5:24, "Enoch walked with God, and he was no longer here, for God took him." To be sure, this information about Enoch is exceedingly sparse, suggesting perhaps God's generous attitude toward such an innocent person. This brief notice in Genesis contrasts sharply with the enormous amount of extrabiblical literature regarding Enoch that extends from the third century BC to the sixth century AD.

Equally enigmatic is the departure of the prophet Elijah for the heavenly realm: "As they [Elijah and Elisha] walked on still conversing, a fiery chariot and fiery horses came between the two of them, and Elijah went up to heaven in a whirlwind" (2 Kgs 2:11). The text does not actually record that Elijah is received into heavenly glory as a fitting reward for his devoted prophetic career. God simply transfers him from earth to his own mysterious dwelling place. As in the case of Enoch, Elijah's exit from human life says very little about the conditions of the afterlife. However, both incidents underline God's enormous power, a power that will ultimately overcome death itself.

Summary

In Mesopotamia and Canaan death is simply accepted as a fact of life. Only the gods (with the exception of Utnaphistim, the Mesopotamian Noah) enjoy the prerogative of eternal life, while humans upon death are consigned to the gloomy netherworld. Though influenced by these cultures, the Old Testament develops its own understanding of death. Death embraces anxiety, illness, and the like. It also appears as a power that resists the divine order of creation. Finally death entails the return of one's life force or energy to God.

Sheol is the biblical counterpart of the Mesopotamian and Canaanite netherworlds. However, the Old Testament sponsors two views about the occupants of Sheol. According to the first view all, both saint and sinner, go to Sheol. According to the second understanding only those who die due to unnatural causes descend to Sheol. However, death due to natural causes can mean the experience of divine blessing when one sleeps with one's ancestors and leaves behind numerous progeny. Hence a sense of community prevails here.

While heaven functions as a firmament holding back a mass of water and as God's dwelling place, the Old Testament provides some intimations of surviving death prior to the indisputable evidence for eternal life in the second century BC. One such intimation is the fate of Enoch and Elijah. In both cases they disappear. In Enoch's case God simply takes him; in Elijah's case God dispatches a chariot of fire and horses of fire with which he ascends to God in a whirlwind. The Old Testament does not attest what happens thereafter.

Reflections

The people of Israel accept death as the surrender of their life force or energy to God. However, in distinguishing between death due to natural causes and that due to unnatural causes, they endow the former with a rich sense of community and continuity. Job, for example, dies full of days in the company of his great-grandchildren (Job 42:16-17). Jacob commands his sons to bury him with his ancestors in the land of Canaan, as he wishes to be gathered to his people (Gen 49:29-30). Although neither Job nor Jacob is moved to a "higher" place, both enjoy divine favor in that their extended family continues on and their name is remembered. Such an understanding of death banishes the sense of loneliness and apartness often associated with "shuffling off this mortal coil." Memory and continuity offset the grim specter of the cessation of the biological processes.

One of the common divine epithets in the Old Testament is "the living God." For example, in Joshua 3:10 Joshua assures the Israelites that the living God is among them when this God routs his people's enemies. In 1 Samuel 17:26 David describes the arrogance of Goliath in these terms: "Who is this uncircumcised Philistine that he should insult the armies of the living God?" This expression conveys the notion that the God of Israel will intervene actively or be clearly present whenever powerful forces threaten the welfare of his people. This living God will not cower in the face of death.

CHAPTER TWO

Further Intimations and Breakthrough

Key Biblical Passages: 2 Maccabees 7; Psalms 16; 49; 73; Wisdom 3; 15:1-6;
Isaiah 25:6-8; 26:7-21; Ezekiel 37:1-14; Daniel 12:1-3;
Hosea 6:1-6

Resurrection as the Restoration of God's People

In the second half of the eighth century BC the prophet Hosea struggles to defeat the religious shallowness of his fellow Israelites. Embroiled in a futile military campaign, the Israelites invoke the intervention of their God in a liturgy of attempted covenant renewal, that is, the renewal of their relationship with God. They depict the Lord as both the source of their problems and the healing power for their restoration. "For it is he who has torn, but he will heal us; / he has struck down, but he will bind our wounds" (Hos 6:1). Here healing is tantamount to reviving since the cure of a seriously ill individual represents bringing a person back to life. The confidence of the petitioners mounts as they continue their liturgy: "He will revive us after two days; / on the third day he will raise us up" (Hos 6:2). The initial language of divine killing followed by the formula of divine restoration on the third day (see 1 Cor 15:4) provides a metaphor of death and resurrection. Such a metaphor is rooted in the notion of God's unlimited power, a power that transcends the insatiable appetite of death. As the Divine Warrior, the God of Israel can thwart *all* enemies.

Preaching to the despondent exiles in Babylon after the fall of Jerusalem in 586 BC, the prophet Ezekiel offers a message of profound hope in the famous vision of the dry bones (37:1-14). He converts the people's lament in 37:11 that their bones are dried up and their hope has vanished into a vision. They have lost the capacity to imagine how things can be turned around and how newness is still possible. His addressees are the dead bones, the victims of crippling despair. The restoration of these bones reveals that God will open their graves and restore them to their homeland. In this process the Lord acts very methodically by providing sinews, then flesh and skin, and finally the breath of life. "I will put sinews on you, make flesh grow over you, cover you with skin, and put breath into you so you may come to life" (Ezek 37:6). This procedure is reminiscent of the various stages in which a baby is formed in the womb: "you fashioned me from clay! . . . With skin and flesh you clothed me, with bones and sinews knit me together" (Job 10:9, 11). In Ezekiel's vision the reassembled and revived dead evoke a type of re-creation. This newly re-created Israel must in the end recognize that their God has acted on their behalf. To sum up, resurrection by means of re-creation is the metaphor of restoration. Not only are those who never existed capable of receiving the gift of life but also those who once lived and then died.

Isaiah 24–27, often labeled the Apocalypse of Isaiah, presents enormous difficulties for interpreters. However, the section dealing with the metaphor of resurrection for restoration (26:7-21) seems to point to a time (perhaps in the fifth century BC) of some national revival after a period of distress. The text reads, "But your dead shall live, their corpses shall rise! / awake and sing, you who lie in the dust!" (26:19). This passage contrasts with 26:13-14, where "other lords" who once controlled Israel are now dead, incapable of any further life. God's final word in this passage is not death but new life (in 26:15 Israel has "increased"). The author of this passage depicts the people's new fertility with the image of dew: "For your dew is a dew of light" (26:19). This revitalization fits well with an earlier statement of hope: "He [the LORD of hosts] will destroy death forever" (25:8). Overall, therefore, these passages in Isaiah 25–26, while they do not clearly articulate belief in the resurrection of the dead, do attest God's enormous power and concern for his people—a concern that will eventually not permit death to enjoy the last word.

Psalms and the Hope for God's Abiding Presence

In addition to resurrection as a metaphor for restoration, another intimation of surviving death emerges from the hope for the abiding enjoyment of God's presence, especially in the Psalms. Psalm 16:10 reads, "For you will not abandon my soul to Sheol, / nor let your devout one see the pit." The main emphasis in the psalm, however, is the focus on God's presence in this life, not the hereafter. Psalm 49:15-16 contrasts the lot of the wicked who are herded into Sheol and that of the righteous one whom the Lord will ransom from Sheol and take to himself. The question naturally arises: where does God take (the same verb is used for Enoch and Elijah) the righteous one? Psalm 73:23-26 also considers the contrast between the righteous and the unrighteous. After viewing the fate of the wicked, the psalmist exclaims, "With your counsel you guide me, and at the end receive me with honor. Whom else have I in the heavens?" (73:24-25). The psalmist has resolved the problem of evil with the assurance that God will right all wrongs. However, as in Psalm 73, the place to which God will take ("receive . . . with honor") the faithful one is admittedly ambiguous. The constant in these psalms is that God will indeed provide the reverse of Sheol. Unfortunately these psalms, while passionately longing for God's abiding presence, offer nothing precise.

Breakthrough

The book of Daniel (written ca. 165 BC) responds to the persecution of faithful Jews by the Seleucid king Antiochus IV Epiphanes. Jews who remain loyal to their faith and resist the enticements of pagan (Hellenistic) culture face death (see 1 Macc 1:54-63). Daniel 7–12 is apocalyptic, that is, a revelatory literature set within a narrative framework in which an otherworldly being (e.g., an angel) discloses something transcendent to a human recipient (here Daniel). In Daniel 12 the angel assures Daniel that the faithful will eventually triumph over their enemies. "Many of those who sleep / in the dust of the earth shall awake; / Some to everlasting life, / others to reproach and everlasting disgrace. / But those with insight shall shine brightly / like the splendor of the firmament, / And those who lead the many to justice / shall be like the stars forever" (12:2-3).

This judgment passage clearly articulates the resurrection of individuals ("sleep" and "awake") from the dead because of its mention of everlasting life. At the same time, however, this passage discusses neither the form of resurrection nor the location of resurrected life.

In addition, it neither anticipates a universal resurrection nor does it specify a resurrection of the body, although this may be implied. Nonetheless the fate of the wise is clear. These wise teachers of the common people ("the many"—see Isa 53:11) seem to include those who suffer martyrdom as well as those who do not. The text notes that these wise will be like the stars (they do not become stars) forever. Since stars are often identified with the angelic host (see Dan 8:10), the implication is that the wise will be associated with angels. The destiny of the wise is similar to Jesus' statement that those who rise from the dead are like angels in heaven (Mark 12:25).

This passage describes the vindication of the faithful through the power of God. Divine justice demands that the fate of the righteous and the unrighteous should be unequivocally distinguished. The result is the reversal of the condition and status of the faithful. The resurrection statement in Daniel 12:2-3 strikes a blow not only for divine omnipotence but also for divine justice. The resurrected ones in this passage reveal God's capacity to respond to loyalty and fidelity.

Like Daniel, 2 Maccabees (perhaps written at the end of the second century BC) also deals with the persecution of Antiochus IV Epiphanes. In 2 Maccabees 7 the author narrates the story of the Maccabean mother and her seven sons as a means of elaborating a theology of martyrdom. The second son boldly states his belief in physical resurrection: "the King of the universe will raise us up to live again forever, because we are dying for his laws" (7:9). The third son states that he hopes to recover his limbs (7:11). Such a physical resurrection is required in order to balance the tortures endured. The mother adds a very distinctive note to this theology of resurrection, namely, the role of creation: "Therefore, since it is the Creator of the universe who shaped the beginning of humankind and brought about the origin of everything, he, in his mercy, will give you back both breath and life" (7:23). Resurrection thus establishes a continuity with creation. The One who gave life in the beginning can restore life at a later point. As in Daniel 12, resurrection functions as divine vindication. The martyrdom of the seven brothers means that God must redress this painful situation. It is worth noting that physical resurrection in 2 Maccabees 7 means restoration to a normal life. In other words, one is not transformed by such a resurrection.

Written in Alexandria, perhaps just before the Christian era, the book of Wisdom has much to say about the afterlife. Persecuted for their religious fidelity, the righteous are judged by the wicked to be utter fools.

However, "[t]he souls of the righteous are in the hand of God, / and no torment shall touch them. / They seemed, in the view of the foolish, to be dead . . . / But they are in peace. . . . / yet is their hope full of immortality" (3:1-4). The righteous are numbered among the sons of God and the holy ones (5:5) and, as in Daniel, enjoy an angelic existence. However, unlike Daniel, the book of Wisdom does not mention resurrection. Instead, this work speaks of being exalted to the heavenly realm. Heavily influenced by Greek, especially Platonic philosophy (see 9:15), the Jewish author of this work envisions immortality as immortality of the soul—it is a product of righteousness: "to know your might is the root of immortality" (15:3). Hand in hand with immortality is incorruptibility. According to Wisdom 2:23 God originally intended humankind for incorruptibility. Incorruptibility is that quality by which the creature resembles the Creator. In sum, immortality of the soul, not resurrection, is Wisdom's foundation for the afterlife.

Other Jewish Voices

This is the period of intertestamental Judaism, a term that refers to the time between 200 BC and 100 AD and to the non-Christian, Jewish works written during that period. What emerges from this rich body of literature is a great variety of beliefs regarding the afterlife. More significantly, there is no single normative Jewish belief about the time, manner, and place of resurrection. The New Testament will reflect this diversity but will differ from the intertestamental writings because of its focus on Jesus.

In 1 Enoch 1–36 ("The Book of the Watchers" stemming from the third century BC) the fall of the angels in Genesis 6:1-4 is viewed as a fall into mortality whereas the ascent of Enoch is a movement toward eternal life. In the so-called Epistle of Enoch (1 Enoch 91–105 from the second century BC) the righteous share the eternal spiritual life of the angels in heaven. Such an existence is neither immortality of the soul nor resurrection of the body. While the bodies of the righteous most likely continue to rest in the earth, a resurrection or exaltation of the spirit to heaven takes place. Probably written just before Daniel and commenting on the same struggle, the book of Jubilees does not appear to endorse a future bodily resurrection. While the bones of the righteous rest in the earth, their spirits will enjoy much joy. A work of the first century BC, the Psalms of Solomon holds that the righteous will rise to eternal life. However, it is not clear whether this work anticipates a bodily resurrection or a revival of one's spirit or soul.

Writing in the first half of the first century BC, the author of 4 Maccabees rewrites 2 Maccabees. Instead of a future resurrection of the body, there is immortality with eternal life beginning at death. Composed after the destruction of Jerusalem in 70 AD, 2 Baruch and 4 Ezra maintain a general resurrection at the conclusion of history. Eventually the righteous will undergo a transformation by means of which they will shine like stars. Such a bodily resurrection will make it possible to recognize the dead. Eventually the body will become luminous in an angelic state.

Qumran or the Dead Sea Scroll community (in existence from the second century BC to the first century AD) provides no unambiguous evidence about bodily resurrection. For these Jews (usually identified as Essenes), upon entrance into the group, one moves into a community that already anticipates heaven. The future thus impinges on the present. By sharing an angelic life within the community, one transcends death and continues that life in heaven.

The Resurrected Jesus as Catalyst

The Jewish world of Palestine, into which Jesus was born, and the Jewish world of the Diaspora (Jews living outside the Holy Land), in which the author of the book of Wisdom flourished, lack a normative belief regarding the afterlife. These worlds of Jewish and Greek (Hellenistic) thought provide no orthodox doctrine regarding the afterlife. However, for Christians the whole worldview changes with the death and resurrection of Jesus of Nazareth. Jesus changes the challenge of death in the transforming experience of Easter Sunday. It is precisely this transformation that Paul of Tarsus will witness on the road to Damascus.

After Easter, Jesus assumes the role as the norm for the relationship between God and humanity. While this God remains the One who brought Israel out of Egypt, this God is now identified as the Father who raised Jesus from death. While Jesus' resurrection facilitates his exaltation as Lord and Judge, it also holds the promise of resurrection and eternal life for believers.

A note of caution. The New Testament does not explicitly discuss the relationship between heaven and the resurrection of the body. In other words, the New Testament does not purposely seek to integrate the resurrection of the body and heavenly existence. To anticipate the following chapters, one may say that two views of heaven exist that are not clearly fused together. First, there is heaven as a place that adapts itself to the popular imagination. For example, Paul speaks in 2 Corinthians 12:2

of being caught up into the third heaven. Second, there is heaven as a higher reality, a state of being, the new world effected by Jesus' glorification. For example, John 6:33 refers to God's bread (the revelation given by Jesus) that comes down from heaven and gives life to the world. As the following chapters will attempt to show, one's existence *in heaven* is *in Christ*. This is a world that transcends the visible, tangible world—it is the "new heaven" and the "new earth" (Rev 21:1). To be in Christ is to share the company of Jesus and believers.

Summary

Further intimations of surviving death include resurrection as the metaphor for the restoration of God's people in the prophets and the hope for abiding enjoyment of God's presence in the book of Psalms. However, the real breakthrough from intimations to clear evidence surfaces in the book of Daniel circa 165 BC. This book speaks of many who will awake to everlasting life, that is, the faithful who suffer persecution will be vindicated. While Daniel does not discuss the form of resurrection, 2 Maccabees, probably written at the end of the second century BC, understands resurrection as restoration to normal life, not transformation. Finally the author of the book of Wisdom in the first century BC sees immortality of the soul, not resurrection, as the foundation of the afterlife.

In considering the intertestamental literature, one discovers a great variety of beliefs regarding the afterlife. In the Jewish world of both Palestine and the Diaspora there is no single normative belief. However, Easter Sunday changes the whole discussion. For believers Jesus' resurrection becomes their norm for understanding eternal life. In this context heaven refers to that state of being or new world effected by Jesus' glorification.

Reflections

Divine justice and the gift of eternal life meet in the book of Daniel. Since loyal Jews are resisting the inroads of Hellenistic influence by clinging to their ancestral faith, God must set things right. He must clearly distinguish between the righteous and the unrighteous. The promise of resurrection for "[m]any of those who sleep / in the dust of the earth" (Dan 12:2) strikes the decisive blow for divine justice. God thus proves that he will respond to loyalty by defeating death. The resurrection of the righteous to eternal life demonstrates the victory of not only divine omnipotence but also divine justice.

The Father's act of raising Jesus from the dead changes the whole discussion of heaven and the afterlife. In a world where multiple divergent views of surviving death abound, the Father's action on Easter Sunday establishes a new criterion or norm for believers. Those who accept Jesus and his message now look to him as the model or exemplar for the meaning of the afterlife. The same Spirit that transforms the dead body of Jesus and thus glorifies him will also be the power that will change them. In Ezekiel 37:10 breath comes into the dead bones and brings them to life. On Easter Sunday the Father sends the Spirit to breathe upon the dead body of Jesus and utterly transform him. The intimations of transcending death in the Old Testament have become a reality in the setting of the empty tomb.

CHAPTER THREE

The Synoptic Gospels and Acts

Key Biblical Passages: Matthew 1:18-25; 8:5-13; 10:26-33; 13:36-43; 25:14-46;
27:51-54; 28:16-20; Mark 9:43-48; 10:17-22; 12:18-27;
16:1-8; Luke 10:17-20; 14:7-14; 16:19-31; 20:27-40;
22:24-30; 23:39-43; 24:13-35; Acts 3:11-26; 4:1-4; 5:27-32;
7:54-60

Introduction

Since Matthew, Mark, and Luke share a common viewpoint or out-look regarding Jesus, they are commonly designated the Synoptic Gos-pels in contradistinction to the Gospel of John that presents a unique approach to Jesus and his ministry. Although the Acts of the Apostles does not qualify as one of the gospels, it is included here since Luke-Acts is a unified work, narrating a single account based on Israel's story and the divine plan of salvation. Thus Acts presupposes the con-tent and focus of the third gospel.

The majority scholarly view is that Mark is the earliest gospel, per-haps written in the late sixties AD. Matthew and Luke, both probably composed between 80 and 90 AD, use Mark as one of their sources. In addition they also employ a source known as "Q" that contains mainly sayings of Jesus not found in Mark (e.g., the Our Father). Matthew and Luke also have their own special sources labeled "M" (e.g., the magi) and "L" (e.g., the shepherds) respectively. There is no clear evidence that Matthew used Luke or vice versa. By observing how these two evangelists use their common sources, one can disengage to some de-gree their theological message.

The Gospel of Mark

In 9:43-48 Mark considers the issue of temptations to sin. (Matthew 18:8-9 offers a simplified account of Mark.) If one's hand (9:43) or one's foot (9:45) causes a person to sin, it is preferable to cut them off and enter into life maimed or lame. If one's eye (9:47) becomes an occasion of sin, it is better to tear it out and enter the kingdom of God with one eye. The pattern in this passage suggests that "life" and "kingdom of God" are equivalent. Hence the life that Jesus is discussing concerns eternal life with God, not merely happiness in this world. Although the passage does not provide specifics about eternal life, it does seem to imply some form of awakening or rising from the dead. The kingdom of God, the very focus of Jesus' mission, at the very least understands "life" as community with God in some way.

In 10:17-22 (see Matt 19:16-22; Luke 18:18-23) Mark tells the story of the rich man who seeks "to inherit eternal life" (10:17). After Jesus' recitation of the commandments, the man acknowledges that he has kept them from his youth. At this point Jesus observes that his questioner lacks one thing, namely, he should sell his possessions and give them to the poor. Jesus then adds, "you will have treasure in heaven; then come, follow me" (10:21). Clearly Jesus is calling the man to discipleship. Unfortunately his great wealth prevents him from accepting Jesus' invitation. According to Mark 3:31-35, disciples, by doing the will of God, become Jesus' brother, sister, and mother. By accepting this call, the rich man would have become a member of Jesus' family. Hence discipleship and familial intimacy with Jesus are interconnected. This would suggest that inheriting eternal life and having treasure in heaven belong to family members.

Undoubtedly the most famous passage in Mark concerning the afterlife is Jesus' debate with the Sadducees about the resurrection in 12:18-27 (see Matt 22:23-33; Luke 20:27-40). As a sect within Judaism, the Sadducees constitute a rather conservative group, denying not only the afterlife but also the existence of angels and revelation apart from the Torah/Pentateuch. To demonstrate the absurdity of an afterlife, especially resurrection, the Sadducees appeal to the levirate law in Deuteronomy 25:5-6 whereby a man is obliged to marry his deceased brother's wife if he leaves no son. The Sadducees propose the case of seven brothers who, in turn, married their sister-in-law without producing a son. At the resurrection, therefore, whose wife will she be since she married all seven brothers (12:23)?

Jesus responds to his opponents by first accusing them of a twofold ignorance, namely, of the Scriptures and of divine power (12:24). Jesus then challenges the basic assumption of his interrogators that human relationships prior to death persist in life after death. After denying this, Jesus asserts that the resurrected are like angels in heaven (12:25). Regarding the Scriptures Jesus refers to the episode of the burning bush and the call of Moses in Exodus 3, noting the thrice repeated phrase "the God of Abraham, the God of Isaac, and the God of Jacob" (Exod 3:6, 15, 16). Jesus concludes this citation with the statement that God is not the "God of the dead but of the living" (12:27).

In this central episode Jesus rejects the following speculative question: How can the body exist in heaven? Instead, he bases hope of the resurrection not on the nature of the human person but on faith in the God of Abraham, Isaac, and Jacob who, though they are dead, are yet alive. Ultimately Jesus grounds his argument on the character of God as a God of the living, not the dead. One is reminded of those passages in the prophets Hosea and Ezekiel that speak of God's power to restore life. One is also challenged to return to Genesis 1–2, where God commands center stage as the source of all life. Finally the notion of community reappears in the mention of the three patriarchs. Resurrection, therefore, involves the regrouping of a family achieved by divine power.

In Mark 16:6 the young man at the tomb says the following to the anointing women: "Do not be amazed! . . . He has been raised; he is not here." The young man's message is directed not only to the terrified women but also to Mark's community. It is probably intended to teach the implications of Jesus' resurrection for fellow Christians who have died before the second coming. What Jesus has experienced his followers will also experience. In brief, Jesus has become the paradigm of life beyond death—an outlook that John and Paul will expand.

The Gospel of Matthew

By way of introduction it is worth noting that one-third of all New Testament uses of the word "heaven" occur in this gospel. Heaven is the place where God the Father has his residence (5:16; 6:9). However, heaven and earth function as parallel places so that the kingdom on earth should reflect the kingdom in heaven. Hence in the Our Father one prays, "your will be done, / on earth as in heaven" (6:10). Significantly Matthew usually qualifies the kingdom as the kingdom of heaven, not the kingdom of God. While many think that Matthew generally employs "heaven" instead of "God" out of respect for the divine name, it is equally plausible that "heaven" constitutes only a stylistic variation. For Matthew, heaven conjures up the idea of God's rule in both the present and the future. As for the future, this rule will usher in the transformation of the world—a paradise in which God's will is fully accomplished.

In addition to the Our Father mentioned above (6:9-13), Matthew's Sermon on the Mount (5:1–7:29) contains other references to heaven. It is the place of one's reward (5:12; see Luke 6:23) as well as the place where believers store up lasting riches that are not exposed to the ravages of nature and the danger of thieves (6:19-21; see Luke 12:33-34). The goal is not to enjoy such treasures in heaven but to let the audience imagine to some degree the experience of eternal life. In 7:13-14 (see Luke 13:24) Jesus urges his audience to enter by the narrow gate that leads to life. As in 6:19-21, by entering through the narrow gate and treading the path to life, believers are preparing for eternal life in the kingdom.

The image of a banquet plays a significant role in Jesus' message about heaven. In 8:11 (see Luke 13:28-29) Jesus announces that Gentiles "will recline with Abraham, Isaac, and Jacob in the kingdom of heaven." In the Old Testament the prophets had already spoken about Gentiles coming to worship the God of Israel in Jerusalem (Isa 2:2-4). Here Matthew heightens the overture to the Gentiles through the image of a banquet. This embraces much more than eating, drinking, and congenial conversation. Dining with the patriarchs captures the status of the guests. Far from being outsiders, the Gentiles have "made" it. Isaiah 25:6 illustrates the power of this image: "On this mountain the LORD of hosts / will provide for all peoples / A feast of rich food and choice wines, / juicy, rich food and pure, choice wines." While Matthew does not venture to explain how these resurrected bodies will function in heaven, the image of a banquet still serves an important purpose.

In his mission sermon in Matthew 10 Jesus exhorts the Twelve to be courageous, even to the point of martyrdom, if necessary. He urges them in these terms: "And do not be afraid of those who kill the body but cannot kill the soul" (10:28). In this exhortation, therefore, Matthew adopts an anthropology in which the soul is one's real self and the body its perishable container. (Luke 12:14 speaks only of the body.) He appears to accept the notion that the disembodied soul can survive physical death and somehow be later reunited with a resurrected body. Such a view reflects the influence of Hellenistic philosophy. As noted earlier, Matthew does not integrate heaven and the activity of resurrected bodies.

In his discourse on the last things ("eschatological") in Matthew 24–25 Jesus underlines the need for disciples to be vigilant when he

returns at the end. In the parable of the ten virgins (25:1-13—unique to Matthew) the wise ones have extra oil with which to trim their lamps while the foolish ones are totally unprepared. When Jesus the bridegroom arrives, the wise ones join him at the wedding feast. Once again the image of a banquet is significant. In the following parable, namely, the talents (25:14-30; see Luke 19:12-27), Jesus is the master who returns after a long time to settle accounts with his servants. The parable clearly deals with Jesus' second coming and the proper behavior expected of disciples. While the third servant is castigated for burying his talent and hence deriving no profit for the master, the first two servants are rewarded for their industry. The master, moreover, says to these servants, "Come, share your master's joy" (25:21, 23). The invitation to joy suggests something like the marriage banquet in the preceding parable. The master and his servants fittingly rejoice together while the unfaithful encounter darkness, weeping, and gnashing of teeth (25:30). In the windup of the kingdom, banquet and joy go hand in hand.

The final scene in Matthew's eschatological discourse is the judgment of the nations (25:31-46—unique to Matthew). At his second coming Jesus will appear as a glorious king in the company of all the angels. Like a shepherd, he separates the sheep (the righteous) from the goats (the unrighteous). Appropriately the sheep enjoy the place of honor at Jesus' right hand while the goats are relegated to his left hand. The criterion of judgment is the identification of Jesus and his family members. To discover Jesus in the hungry, thirsty, and so forth, and to assist them is to enter the kingdom: "Come, you who are blessed by my Father. Inherit the kingdom prepared for you from the foundation of the world " (25:34). This passage recalls the blessing of the patriarchs, for example, Jacob in Genesis 48:15-16. Linked with blessing is the conferral of inheritance. There is also continuity with creation. God's purpose here in the end does not differ from that in the beginning. As the episode concludes, Jesus' righteous family members enter into eternal life (25:46). Eternal life is nothing less than a family celebration.

In the passion narrative Matthew offers a unique interpretation of the effects of Jesus' death (27:51-53). Like Mark, Matthew mentions the rending of the temple curtain (27:51). However, he goes on to narrate other portents that reveal the impact of his death: the shaking of the earth, the splitting of rocks, the opening of tombs, the raising of many bodies of the saints, the exiting from their tombs, their entry into Jerusalem, and their appearance to many (27:51-53). In short, the death of Jesus has cosmic consequences. Drawing from Ezekiel 37, namely, the restoration of the dry bones to life, Matthew has converted the prophet's vision into a reality. The turning point of the ages is the death of Jesus, not his resurrection. Hence the resurrection of the saints is tied to Jesus' death.

However, Matthew issues a disclaimer. In 27:53 he corrects the confusion of the events just narrated. He writes, "And coming forth from their tombs *after his resurrection*, they entered the holy city" (emphasis added). With this disclaimer he connects the resurrection of the saints to both the death *and* resurrection of Jesus. Now it is the death-resurrection that ushers in the new age. Moreover, Matthew's use of the earthquake in 27:51 is tied to the account of Jesus' resurrection in 28:2: "And behold, there was a great earthquake . . . " Matthew thus concludes that Jesus, through his death and resurrection, has become the paradigm of the afterlife. For believers, life after death hinges on Jesus' death and the transformed life of his resurrection.

The Gospel of Luke

The third gospel shares certain motifs with Matthew and Mark. In Luke 10 the third evangelist narrates the mission of the seventy-two. Upon their return Jesus urges them not to rejoice over their power to defeat demons but to "rejoice because your names are written in heaven" (10:20). Hence it is much more important to have one's name entered into the census list of heaven than in that of earth. In the parable about the conduct of guests and hosts (the dais scramblers, etc.) in 14:7-14 Jesus teaches his followers to avoid a tit-for-tat mentality. When inviting guests, they should consider not only those who can return the favor but also the poor, the crippled, the lame, and the blind. He adds, "you will be repaid at the resurrection of the righteous" (14:14). At the time of the resurrection God will provide proper retribution for their guest lists. At the Last Supper Jesus exhorts the Twelve to persevere with him in his trials. As a reward for such perseverance, they will "eat and drink at *my* table in *my* kingdom . . . " (22:30, emphasis added). The image of a banquet appears once again. However, Jesus heightens the dimension of intimacy by stressing "my" table and "my" kingdom.

While Luke accepts the resurrection associated with Jesus' second coming, he also introduces passages that reveal the reward of heaven immediately after death. In the well-known parable of the rich man and Lazarus (16:19-31—unique to Luke), "[w]hen the poor man died, he was carried away by angels to the bosom of Abraham" (16:22). In the next verse Abraham has Lazarus by his side. The image of a banquet surfaces once again with Lazarus enjoying the place of honor at Abraham's right side. Thus Lazarus's new life begins immediately after death. Some would describe such a mode of being as a disembodied existence in an intermediate state, that is, one of waiting for the general resurrection. In any event Luke underlines the primacy of community and intimacy, namely, Lazarus *with* Abraham.

Another scene that illustrates the same idea of heavenly reward immediately after death is the account of the so-called Good Thief (23:39-43). This criminal addresses Jesus as a king since he asks to be remembered when Jesus comes into his kingdom. To this request Jesus responds, "Amen, I say to you, today you will be with me in Paradise" (23:43). In light of this reply the criminal will share in Christian destiny since he will join Jesus in the abode of the righteous. As in the case of Lazarus, Luke does not spell out the criminal's mode of existence after death. However, he again signals the profound sense of community by his use of the phrase "with me."

Does Luke provide any hints about the condition of a resurrected body? Unlike Paul, who considers this question explicitly in 1 Corinthians 15, Luke does not address it directly. However, in his account of the travelers on the road to Emmaus (24:13-35) he may provide a few clues. Almost at the beginning of the episode Luke states emphatically that it is Jesus himself (24:15). However, he is not initially recognized as himself (24:16). Jesus begins to interpret the Scriptures for them and gives the impression of walking on ahead (24:28-30). He then gives in to the travelers' request by breaking bread with them. At this point he is recognized but vanishes (24:31). It is indeed the same Jesus but he is no longer as he was—his reality has changed. In a word, the same person Jesus has been transformed. In this episode, therefore, Luke may be obliquely discussing the resurrected bodies of believers. They will be the same persons but they will be transformed.

The Acts of the Apostles

In his speech before King Agrippa Luke has Paul proclaim that Jesus is the first to rise from the dead (26:23). Elsewhere Luke explains the significance of Jesus' primary role by the use of titles. In 3:15 Peter announces in a speech in the temple that his audience asked for a murderer (Barabbas) and killed the author of life but God reversed this heinous act by raising Jesus from the dead. The title "author" connotes "trailblazer"—Jesus is the one who has opened up the way to eternal life. Luke thus intends a contrast: Jesus is the one who gives life while the murderer takes it away. In Peter's speech before the Sanhedrin Luke emphasizes Jesus' exaltation at God's right hand (5:31), using the titles "leader" and "savior." The resurrection of Jesus, therefore, impacts all believers. Jesus confers this life on them since he has originated such life in his resurrection. His resurrection influences all his sisters and brothers.

In Acts 4, while the apostles Peter and John are preaching in the temple, the Sadducees and others confront them, annoyed that the apostles are proclaiming in Jesus the resurrection of the dead. The phrase "resurrection of the dead" (4:2) and the presence of the Sadducees alert the reader that Luke is referring back to Jesus' discussion with the Sadducees in Luke 20:27-40. By introducing changes into Mark's text, Luke adds new aspects about the meaning of resurrection. In Luke 20:35 Jesus points out, "but those who are deemed worthy to attain to the coming age and to the resurrection from the dead neither marry nor are given in marriage." While Mark 12:25 observes that they are like angels, Luke adds that they are "the children of God because they are the ones who will rise" (20:36). While Mark 12:27 notes that the God of the patriarchs is God not of the dead but of the living, Luke notes, "for to him all are alive" (20:38).

By reechoing this passage, Acts 4 changes the focus to ask about the relevance of God, not the fate of believers. To be the God of Abraham, Isaac, and Jacob is to be the God of living persons. The reality of the resurrection resides in God, in his power and love. Whoever belongs to God must live. The apostles, therefore, in Acts 4 are teaching Jesus' view on the resurrection of the dead. All who repent and are found worthy will participate in eternal life.

As in the case of Lazarus and the Good Thief, Luke also narrates another instance of immediate union with God after death. In Acts 7 he presents a very long passage about Stephen, the first martyr. Having infuriated his enemies, Stephen looks up to heaven and sees the glory of God and Jesus standing at the right hand of God (7:55). He adds, "Behold, I see the heavens opened and the Son of Man standing at the right hand of God" (7:56). While they are stoning Stephen, he prays after the manner of Jesus in Luke 23:46: "Lord Jesus, receive my spirit" (7:59). The posture of Jesus (standing rather than sitting at God's right hand) seems to symbolize his welcoming Stephen into heaven (see Luke 21:36). In sum, Luke describes Stephen's immediate union with God and Jesus, although he does not discuss the mode of Stephen's heavenly existence.

Summary

In the Synoptics and Acts eternal life means community *with* God. The image of a banquet, especially the wedding banquet, captures this dimension of intimacy. The notion of being Jesus' extended family also underlines the close bonds that exist there. Eternal life also implies a special relationship with Jesus. In Luke 22:30, for example, the Twelve will eat and drink at Jesus' table in his kingdom. Similarly, Jesus assures the Good Thief that he will enjoy his company in paradise (Luke 23:43). Eternal life also connotes a radical change of existence. Although such a change is not spelled out in full detail, there are a few clues. Thus those who experience the resurrection become like angels. As such, they cannot die anymore (Luke 20:36). Matthew 13:43 intimates this transformation in these terms: "Then [at the end of the age] the righteous will shine like the sun in the kingdom of their Father."

A final note. The Synoptics and Acts root this transformation process in the resurrection of Jesus. As first to rise from the dead, he is hailed the trailblazer or originator of life. As the following chapters will show, John and Paul will exploit the primacy of Jesus in the shaping of the afterlife. Ultimately one must confess the presence of the God of surprises in the resurrection of Jesus. As Acts 3:15 brusquely puts it, "The author of life you put to death, but God raised him from the dead." Hence this God has the capacity to take what is evil (the killing of an innocent person) and convert it into something good (exaltation through resurrection). To explore the New Testament notions of the afterlife is to admit a God of reversals. The cross and the empty tomb speak of a God of power but also of a God of love.

Reflections

He is the same, but he is different! He is transformed, but he is still Jesus! These statements perhaps capture Luke's understanding of the resurrection in his account of the walk to Emmaus. Although Luke initially states that it is Jesus who joins up with the travelers (24:15), they do not immediately recognize him (24:16). Only at the breaking of the bread (24:31) are their eyes opened. Luke seems to be suggesting that the resurrection of believers will follow the pattern of the "trailblazer." They will retain their personal identities but they will be different. They will not shed their personal selves but they will be transformed. The model for the resurrection of believers is and must be Jesus himself.

Matthew sees the death and resurrection of Jesus as one event comprising two episodes (there is an earthquake in each). His death provokes the earthquake, the splitting of rocks, and so forth. It thus represents the start of the turning point of the ages. With his disclaimer in 27:53 Matthew observes that many bodies of the saints exit their tombs only *after* Jesus' resurrection. For Matthew, therefore, the after-life hinges on both the death and the resurrection of Jesus. To enter into Jesus' resurrection, believers must not bypass the scene on Calvary. To embrace the resurrected Lord, one must first acknowledge the crucified Jesus.

In his infancy narrative Matthew explains Mary's virginal conception by citing the Greek text of Isaiah 7:14. However, he also adds the meaning of the name "Emmanuel" for Jesus, namely, "God is *with* us" (1:23, emphasis added). Although the concept of community with Jesus appears in many gospel narratives, only Matthew spells out this being *with* by means of a title or name. Matthew also reveals the central role of this title or name in the very last verse of his gospel: "And behold, I am *with* you always, until the end of the age" (28:20, emphasis added). By this inclusion (the device of repeating the same word, phrase, etc., used in the beginning at the end) Matthew has unified his entire gospel under the aegis of presence. The risen Lord has not left his community at all—he is still there, providing hope for those who yearn to meet him in heaven.

The sense of extended family and the following of the "trailblazer" complement each other. All three Synoptic writers identify disciples as members of Jesus' own family. To this familial bond Luke in Acts adds the role of Jesus as trailblazer, namely, the one who opens up the path to eternal life through his resurrection. In this capacity Jesus functions as the head of the household who invites his family members to join him on the journey that leads through death to eternal life. As trail-blazer, Jesus continues to provide.

CHAPTER FOUR

The Gospel of John

Key Biblical Passages: John 3:1-36; 5:19-30; 6:35-59; 7:37-39; 10:1-30; 11:17-27;
12:20-36; 15:1-17; 17:1-8

Introduction

Whereas the Synoptics emphasize Jesus' proclamation of the kingdom, the Fourth Gospel insists that Jesus is the Word who has come from the Father. John focuses on revelation, specifically the Son's revelation to the world of what he has both seen and heard in the presence of the Father. To express it another way, Jesus is the Great Communicator between heaven and earth. Moreover, Jesus is so intimately linked to God that this gospel asserts in its opening verse that the Word is indeed God. Similarly, toward the end of the gospel Thomas will address Jesus as "My Lord and my God!" (20:28).

This gospel was probably written between 90 and 100 AD. After the prologue (1:1-18), the first half (1:19–12:50) recounts how Jesus, having communicated his Father's message, is rejected by the world. The second half (13:1–20:29) narrates the Son's return to the Father by means of his death on the cross, an event, not of shame and ignominy, but of glorification. (John 21, while part of the text of this gospel, seems to have been written at a later date.) From beginning to end Jesus is a divine person who reveals his intimate relationship with the Father ("The Father and I are one" [10:30]) to the world.

To anticipate, the notions of heaven and resurrection from the dead differ from those in the Synoptics. The Fourth Gospel underlines the *present* experience of salvation. Believers already enjoy eternal life because they believe that Jesus is the incarnate One: "whoever hears my word and believes in the one who sent me has eternal life" (5:24). Hence the resurrection of believers from the dead merely continues the eternal life that Jesus has granted.

Eternal Life: Present yet Future

In the discourse following the conversation with Nicodemus (3:11-21) Jesus states categorically that only he can reveal heavenly things since only he has come down from heaven (3:31, 34). To believe that Jesus has been lifted up (Jesus' crucifixion *and* exaltation) is to gain eternal life (3:14-15). Developing the notion of salvation, Jesus teaches that the goal of the Father's sending of his only Son into the world is eternal life for believers. As the end of John 3 puts it, "Whoever believes in the Son has eternal life" (3:36).

In the discourse following a cure on the Sabbath (5:19-30) Jesus defends his right to work on the Jewish day of rest. Here he presents eternal life as both present and future. In 5:24 believers already possess eternal life: "whoever hears my word and believes in the one who sent me has eternal life and . . . has passed from death to life." This passage from death to life is not a future-oriented promise. Rather, it is happening now. Hence the enjoyment of eternal life does not start after death. Because eternal life is God's life (5:26), it is not subject to delay and dissolution.

There is still a tension in this passage. While believers have already passed from death to life (see 1 John 3:14), they know only too well of the grim reality of the everyday experience of death. In 5:28-29 Jesus professes acceptance of the time when the dead in their graves will hear his voice and exit their tombs. Those who have done good will come out to enjoy the resurrection of life. Hence those who have eternal life now must still cope with the reality of physical death and anticipate the summons to leave their tombs for the resurrection of life.

Believers encounter an enormous paradox in this passage. While they already possess eternal life, they do not experience the resurrection immediately—that event still lies in the future. Nonetheless believers must demonstrate the courage to see beyond physical life and embrace a future contingent on their response to Jesus' word. This is the dilemma of "already" but "not yet." Eternal life has already begun but the full enjoyment of that life in the resurrection has not yet taken place. There appears to be a detour of sorts between heaven and earth.

The Bread of Life

In 6:35-58 John presents his discourse on the bread of life that consists of two parts. In the first part (6:35-50) the heavenly bread is Jesus' revelation or teaching. In the second part (6:51-58) this bread is the Eucharist. While this gospel, unlike the Synoptics, does not have Jesus institute the Eucharist at the Last Supper, it does develop the significance of the Eucharist in 6:51-58, a chapter that opens with the multiplication of the loaves and fish (6:1-15). John, therefore, has added this second part as a parallel to the first, enriching the theme of heavenly bread from the perspective of the Eucharist.

In the revelatory first part of the discourse (6:35-50) the paradox of eternal life as present yet future returns. John 6:47-48 captures the present dimension: "whoever believes has eternal life. I am the bread of life." John 6:40, 44 focuses on the future aspect, namely, that believers will be raised on the last day. As the Word who has come down from heaven, Jesus offers his revelation as nourishment that enables believers to eat and not die (6:50). This eternal life is God's very own life that Jesus lives as the Word. However, believers also share in this life before and after death. Hence eternal life is not some vague quality or aspect conferred on believers. Rather, believers in their entire being are divinely alive.

In the eucharistic second part of the discourse (6:51-58) this living bread is Jesus' own flesh: "the bread that I will give is my flesh for the life of the world" (6:51). Eucharist articulates the belief that Jesus has not only become flesh (human) but has also given his flesh and blood as food and drink that nourishes believers. It is vitally important to realize that flesh and blood are not parts of Jesus. Flesh means the entire person as mortal and natural. Blood designates the whole person as living. Together flesh and blood signifies the living human person. Here as well, the twofold aspect of eternal life surfaces once again: "Whoever eats my flesh and drinks my blood has eternal life, and I will raise him up on the last day" (6:54). To celebrate Eucharist is to establish a bond that unites Jesus and believers (6:56).

Eternal life, baptism, and Eucharist form a unity for believers. While baptism bestows the life that the Father shares with Jesus, Eucharist is the food that sustains and nourishes that life. Eucharist celebrates the self-giving of Jesus that makes eternal life possible. Eucharist strengthens believers, not as isolated individuals, but as members of a community whose destiny is ongoing life with God and one another. Eucharist provides the food necessary to experience heaven.

The Good Shepherd and His Sheep

On the occasion of the feast of the Dedication (Hanukkah) Jesus addresses the issue of his status as Messiah (10:25-30). Although he has already responded to his opponents' questions about this matter under the image of the Good Shepherd (10:1-18), they still have not listened. In 10:25-30, therefore, Jesus returns to this imagery. Whereas his followers hear his voice and follow him, his opponents do not because they are not his sheep (10:27-28).

At this point Jesus enumerates the qualities of his sheep in addition to hearing and following. They possess eternal life so that they will never perish and no one will snatch them away from their Shepherd (10:28). The sheep cannot be snatched because the life that believers receive from Jesus is ultimately rooted in his Father. Since no power surpasses that of God, believers' union with God is guaranteed (10:29). In 10:30 Jesus solemnly affirms, "The Father and I are one."

Here the whole question of the afterlife hinges on the intimate bond that connects the Father, Jesus, and believers. Ultimately it is a question of relationships, hence of community. The eternal life that believers receive now comes from Jesus who not only grants life but is life itself (11:25; 14:6). In turn, the life that Jesus enjoys comes from his Father. Jesus, therefore, represents the complete victory of life over death because of his unique ties to the Father. Believers can look for the consummation of eternal life in the resurrection because of this sharing in the Father-Son relationship. Heaven is grounded in family ties.

The Raising of Lazarus

In 11:17-27 John narrates the encounter between Jesus and Martha following the death of her brother Lazarus four days earlier. Upon meeting Jesus, Martha acknowledges him as a miracle worker, that is, if Jesus had been available earlier, her brother would not have died (11:22). Her conviction is based on the fact that God will not refuse Jesus anything. At this point Martha's faith, like that of Nicodemus (3:2) and the man born blind (9:31-32), is clearly limited. Jesus, however, goes on to reassure Martha that Lazarus will rise (11:23). Professing a common Jewish teaching on the resurrection of the dead on the last day, Martha interprets Jesus' remark to mean not rising now but only at the end. Jesus reacts to this profession by saying, "I am the resurrection and the life; whoever believes in me, even if he dies, will live, and everyone who lives and believes in me will never die" (11:25-26). Jesus concludes by directly asking Martha whether she believes him.

This scene in John is calculated to respond to the community's problem, that is, if to believe in Jesus means to possess eternal life now, how can one explain the death of faithful disciples? Lazarus thus becomes the faithful disciple who has died and Martha represents the community that must respond to the challenge of believing in Jesus as the resurrection and the life. Jesus' self-revelation as the resurrection and the life is this gospel's reply to the community's problem. In effect, Jesus is saying that belief in him is indeed the only way to resurrection and life. Faith in Jesus confers life both now and hereafter (see 5:25, 27-29). Jesus *is* the resurrection and the life, and the eternal life he gives to believers transcends physical death but without eliminating it. In dealing with the death of others and one's own death, disciples must continue to be anchored in Jesus' self-revelation.

To accept Jesus as the resurrection and the life is not to reject the reality of physical death. Believers must not deny it or downplay it. Rather, believers are challenged to see physical death as a stage in the eternal life bestowed by Jesus: "whoever believes in me, even if he dies, will live" (11:25). Disciples must view Jesus as the paradigm of this from-death-to-life transition. According to John the cross becomes Jesus' throne, the moment of his glorification as the Son of the Father: "And when I am lifted up from the earth, I will draw everyone to myself" (12:32). While Jesus fully experiences physical death, that death is birth into glory. In 19:34 John mentions the blood and water flowing from the side of Jesus, symbolizing the reality of his death (blood) and the gift of the Spirit (water). Since death by crucifixion has led to glorification, Jesus is now able to bestow the Spirit on the community (7:38-39).

It is good to remember that the raising of Lazarus (11:44), like that of the daughter of Jairus (Matt 9:25; Mark 5:42; Luke 8:55) and the son of the widow of Nain (Luke 7:15), involves revivification or resuscitation. The person so raised is brought back to life with the expectation of dying again. The raising of Jesus as well as that of the faithful is quite distinct. Such a raising is that act by which God transforms his son Jesus and the faithful and thereby conquers death. This raising is also different from the anticipated resurrection of the Maccabean brothers in 2 Maccabees 7. Their hope is to be raised to their previous state in which their bodies will be restored.

The Grain of Wheat

In this scene that focuses on Jesus' "hour" (12:20-26) Jesus reacts to the news that some Greeks would like to see him. John links the arrival of these first Gentiles ("Greeks") to Jesus' statement about the arrival of his "hour": "The hour has come for the Son of Man to be glorified" (12:23). In John the "hour" sums up the entire salvific process of death, resurrection, and ascension. In the face of such universalism ("Greeks") Jesus is prepared to lay down his life.

The powerful image of the grain of wheat (12:24) that remains merely itself unless it falls into the ground captures the theme of Jesus' death: "unless a grain of wheat falls to the ground and dies, it remains just a grain of wheat." Jesus then adds the image of gathering, that is, if it dies, it yields much fruit. Jesus is thus explaining that his death will effect life for all, more precisely that only death brings life. Hence those who seek eternal life must also be ready like Jesus to put their lives on the line. Jesus expresses this truth by contrasting love/lose and hate/keep. Whereas whoever loves his life loses it, "whoever hates his life in this world will preserve it for eternal life" (12:25). The willingness to let go, therefore, reaps the harvest of a full life both here and hereafter. In 12:26 Jesus adds that the disciples must follow him like servants and be where their master Jesus is. The outcome of such unflagging service is the honor the Father will bestow.

This passage provides a poignant lesson in the strategy of loss and gain. By losing oneself (the grain of wheat falling into the ground), one gains a bountiful harvest (much fruit). To be sure, the shadow of the cross falls over both Jesus and believers. However, in embracing the cross like Jesus, disciples can be exalted. The significance of community emerges once again.

Exaltation for faithful disciples is aptly expressed in the notion of the honor conferred by the Father. The Father honors the servant who has served his Son so well. The eternal life that begins by accepting Jesus and following him even to the point of death, if necessary, culminates in the continuation of eternal life in the company of the Father and Jesus. Although heaven entails endless sacrifice and unstinting service, it leads to ongoing community, namely, being with the Father and Jesus as well as their extended family.

Abiding in Jesus and the Commandment to Love

John 13:1–17:26 constitutes Jesus' last discourse. As the moment for his departure to the Father approaches, Jesus gathers his disciples one more time, loving them to the very end (13:1). Although this section contains various components (narrative, discourse, prayer), it enjoys a fundamental unity. As a farewell discourse, that is, a speech given by a hero approaching death that deals with the future concerns of the community (see, e.g., Jacob in Gen 49:1-28), this section fits well into the overall plan of the gospel. John 15:1-17, as part of the larger discourse, emphasizes two themes: (1) abiding in Jesus (15:1-11), and (2) the commandment to love (15:12-17).

Abiding in Jesus opens with the parable of the vine and the branches (15:1-6) with certain allegorical elements (Father = vine grower; Jesus = vine; disciples = branches). Against this background Jesus as the vine claims to be the one who brings genuine life from the Father. Not to bear fruit is not to share in the life/vine and hence to be dead (15:6). However, to share in that life is to share it with others: "and everyone that does [bear fruit] he prunes so that it bears more fruit" (15:2). The cleansing word of Jesus (15:3) requires a response, namely, abiding/living on in Jesus (15:4). Productivity is essential in this personal, intimate union.

In 15:7-11 John emphasizes the verb "to abide." Union with Jesus is based on his word or revelation (15:7). The Father is glorified in the disciples who continue the mission of the Son (15:8). In 15:9 John introduces the theme of love that is linked to abiding in Jesus' love that, in turn, originates in the Father's love. To abide means to acknowledge Jesus' love by keeping his commandments just as Jesus has kept his Father's commandments. The disciples' union with Jesus produces joy, indeed a complete joy (15:11).

In 15:12-17 the commandment to love takes center stage. Mutual love flows from Jesus' love of the disciples that derives from the Father's love for Jesus. The model for such love is Jesus' death for others (15:12). This love constitutes the circle of Jesus' intimates who are privy to the word Jesus received from the Father (15:15). Jesus' choice of such intimates has this goal in mind: "to go and bear fruit that will remain" (15:16). The fitting conclusion to this section is "love one another" (15:17).

According to the Synoptics, disciples of Jesus become his brother, sister, and mother (Matt 12:50; Mark 3:35; Luke 8:21). In John, however, the bond between Jesus and believers is much deeper and more intimate like a branch that draws life from the vine. To abide in Jesus is to abide in the Father—the typical Johannine relationship. However, such abiding also embraces others since disciples are commanded to go and bear fruit. Such productivity becomes manifest in mutual love. For John, therefore, eternal life implies the ongoing reality of abiding in Jesus and hence abiding in the Father. Such eternal life necessarily possesses community implications because of the reality of mutual love. Heaven, therefore, implies an ever deepening, intimate relationship begun on earth. Such eternal life is nothing less than the eternal love grounded in the vine and the vine grower.

Jesus' Final Prayer

In 17:1-8 Jesus prays to the Father for his own glorification and refers to his mission of glorifying him by fulfilling the task of making him known. Although Jesus' exaltation has not yet occurred, one senses that he has already ascended to the Father and that the disciples are privy to this private exchange. The use of the title "Father" (17:1, 5) heightens the intimacy of this exchange.

In 17:1-2 after asking the Father to glorify him, Jesus acknowledges that he glorifies the Father by giving eternal life to the disciples. John 17:3 clarifies this notion of eternal life: "that they should know you, the only true God, and the one whom you sent, Jesus Christ." Thus knowing the God revealed by Jesus in his words and works gives life. While knowledge of God in the Old Testament means obedience to God's will (in Hosea 6:6 steadfast love = knowledge of God), it also connotes intimacy and immediate experience. For John, the disciples already enjoy such eternal life/knowledge.

After petitioning the Father for the glory he enjoyed prior to creation itself (17:5), Jesus attests that he has made God's name known to the disciples (17:6). This passage stresses the disciples' intimacy and personal experience of God since to reveal the name is to communicate everything that can be known about the reality of God. As a result of that revelation, the disciples realize that everything Jesus has—his message—comes from the Father.

In this passage John sums up the very core of eternal life by speaking of knowledge. This is not an exercise in purely abstract, cerebral knowledge. Rather, such knowledge focuses on the Father and the Son. Knowing them adds a very profound dimension of intimacy to the notion of eternal life. The human experience of truly knowing another person captures to a limited degree the welcoming embrace of the Father and the Son in sharing themselves with believers. To that extent knowledge goes hand in hand with love. As one gets to know another person on a deeper level, one is prepared to love on a higher level. Heaven presupposes a community open to the intimacy of such knowledge.

Summary

The Gospel of John teaches that eternal life involves a tension, that is, it is present yet future. While believers have already passed from death to life, they know only too well the grim reality of physical death. To sustain disciples on their journey, the Fourth Gospel highlights the role of the Eucharist. Jesus has given his flesh and blood as the food and drink that nourishes believers. He assures them that they have eternal life and that he will raise them up on the last day. As the Good Shepherd, Jesus teaches his sheep that in possessing eternal life they will never perish or be snatched away from him. In the raising of Lazarus, Jesus goes so far as to say that he himself is the resurrection and the life. He exhorts his disciples to see physical death as a stage in the eternal life he bestows.

In the parable of the grain of wheat Jesus speaks not only of his death for all but also of the need to obtain eternal life by being willing to sacrifice one's own life. Like servants, disciples must follow Jesus and be where he is. By losing themselves, they gain a fruitful harvest. In the parable of the vine and the branches Jesus focuses on the close bond existing between himself and his disciples. This bond, in turn, demands that they bear fruit for others. They must abide in Jesus and thus abide in his love that originates in the Father's love. Such abiding manifests itself in mutual love. In his final prayer Jesus identifies eternal life as knowing the Father and Jesus whom he has sent. Such knowledge is an intimate, personal experience. The eternal life that begins on earth culminates in an ever deeper awareness of the Father and the Son.

Reflections

For John, eternal life begins here and now with the acceptance of Jesus' message from the Father. Hence believers are divinely alive with the life of Jesus and his Father. While the journey to eternal life has already begun, its total reality still lies in the future. Paradoxically believers transcend the reality of death but without eliminating it. To deal with this paradox, John presents Jesus as the living bread. To share in the Eucharist is to have eternal life and to look forward to resurrection on the last day.

Jesus' response to Martha that he himself is the resurrection and the life is both comforting and challenging. It is comforting in that Jesus himself embodies the human yearning to survive beyond death. Jesus, therefore, is the only way to eternal life. It is challenging in that Jesus achieves his exaltation by being lifted up from the earth. Hence believers cannot attain the glory of the resurrection without the pain of the cross. Death is birth into glory.

For John, eternal life is not a narcissistic enterprise comprising only the Father, Jesus, and the isolated individual. Rather, eternal life is unabashedly communal. The goal of the branches' intimacy with the vine is to bear fruit, indeed fruit that will last. John sums up such lasting fruit with the command to love one another. In the grain of wheat analogy believers gather much fruit only by dying. Only by losing themselves for others, will they gain a bountiful harvest.

On the other hand, one must not exclude the dimension of personal intimacy in the notion of eternal life. John encapsulates such intimacy with the term "knowledge," namely, knowing the Father and the Son. It is a knowledge that embraces love. To know a person on a deeper level is to love such a person on a higher level. For believers, such knowing/loving has already happened.

CHAPTER FIVE

Paul

Part I

Key Biblical Passages: 1 Corinthians 6:12-20; 15:1-58; Galatians 2:15-21; 3:23-29; 6:11-16; Philippians 1:12-16; 3:2-21; 1 Thessalonians 4:13-18

Introduction

Paul adopts a theological approach different from that of the Synoptics and John. Whereas the Synoptics employ narratives underlining the proclamation of the kingdom of God and whereas John recounts Jesus' ministry focusing on his revelation from the Father, Paul goes his own way on two counts. First, instead of narratives, Paul communicates his message in a series of letters. Second, Paul opts to rivet his attention on God's saving work in Jesus' death and resurrection. As a result, Paul displays little interest in the ministry of Jesus, including his miracles. Paul argues that he truly knows who Jesus is by looking through the prism of his death and resurrection. Although aware of some of Jesus' specific teachings, for example, divorce in 1 Corinthians 7:10-11, his point of departure in addressing issues and motivating his communities is the cross linked to the resurrection. Thus in Romans 4:25 he speaks of the Lord Jesus "who was *handed over* for our transgressions and was *raised* for our justification."

When Luke recounts Paul's Damascus experience on three occasions in Acts, he notes that there is a great light (9:3; 22:6; 26:13) and that Paul

37

hears Jesus' voice (9:4; 22:7; 26:14). His traveling companions hear the voice but see no one in 9:7. In 22:9 they see the light but hear no one. Finally in 26:13 they see the light but are not said to hear the voice. According to Luke, therefore, Paul does not actually see Jesus. However, in 1 Corinthians 15:8 Paul categorically states that he actually saw the Lord (see also 1 Cor 9:1). In Galatians 1:16 he declares that God revealed his Son to him. It is this unique personal experience that sets Paul apart from the evangelists, since only he personally encounters the risen One. In turn, this overwhelming experience shapes whatever he writes about the afterlife and the general resurrection. For Paul, it is heaven via Damascus.

Of the thirteen letters attributed to Paul in the canon, seven are generally regarded by scholars as genuine letters, namely, Romans, 1–2 Corinthians, Galatians, Philippians, 1 Thessalonians, and Philemon (all probably written in the fifties). The other six letters, though they bear the name of Paul, are not written by him and are usually labeled Deutero-Pauline. Ephesians and Colossians appear to be the work of disciples of Paul who develop new themes beyond Paul's theology. The Pastoral Letters (1–2 Timothy and Titus) envision a more evolved church structure and focus on church order and preservation of the deposit of faith. Finally 2 Thessalonians may stem from an author who invokes Paul's authority in dealing with issues about the second coming. The procedure in this chapter is to present four of the genuine letters of Paul in their probable chronological order (1 Thessalonians, Galatians, Philippians, and 1 Corinthians). The next chapter will consider 2 Corinthians and Romans as well as letters by interpreters of Paul (Colossians and Ephesians).

I Thessalonians

In 4:13-18 Paul responds to a question raised by the Christian Thessalonian community. This community is troubled about the fate of Christians who have already died, specifically about whether or not they will be excluded from salvation at the second coming of Jesus. Belief in Jesus' imminent return provides some of the background to this question. In reply, Paul lays out a four-point scenario regarding the second coming and the resurrection of the dead. First, at the second coming the Lord will descend from heaven. Here Paul adds the apocalyptic stage props for the event: a cry of command, the archangel's call, and the sound of the trumpet (4:16). Second, the dead in Christ will rise first (4:16). Third, those still alive will be snatched up in the clouds along with the resurrected faithful to meet the Lord in the air (4:17). Fourth, the outcome will be everlasting union with the Lord (4:17).

Paul draws an important connection between the death and resurrection of Jesus and the resurrection of believers: "For if we believe that Jesus died and rose, so too will God, through Jesus, bring with him those who have fallen asleep" (4:14). Belief in the death and resurrection of Jesus provides the basis for hope that the dead will also rise. Admittedly Paul does not develop to any great extent the link between Jesus' death and resurrection and the resurrection of believers, such as he will do in 1 Corinthians 15. However, he attests unequivocally to a union between Jesus and believers. Hence the reality of community does not recede into the background. Death cannot separate believers from Christ.

At the same time Paul leaves some issues unanswered. Will believers who go out to meet the Lord return with him to earth or will he bring them to heaven? How will the human body participate in eternal life? In this earliest of his letters, therefore, Paul does not attempt a solution, especially regarding the second question. At this stage he seems content to state the fact of the resurrection without going into details. At this moment the question of eternal life with all its particulars belongs to an unseen reality unobservable to human scrutiny. In fairness to Paul one must concede that his letters are occasional, that is, directed to precise problems and concerns. In 1 Thessalonians Paul has seemingly limited himself to the question of the fate of the dead at the general resurrection and the second coming of Jesus. In 1 Corinthians 15 he will address the issue of the resurrection body specifically.

Despite such limitations, Paul touches on the centrality of community. Here the relatively simple preposition "with" plays a significant role. After being snatched up in the clouds to meet the Lord, "we shall always be *with* the Lord" (4:17). The phrase emphasizes the sense of a vital union with Jesus. In other words, to live in the company of Jesus constitutes eternal life. In this same passage Paul directs attention to another dimension of community, namely, that of other believers. In 4:17 he mentions that those alive at the second coming will join the company of the resurrected dead: those "who are left, will be caught up together *with* them in the clouds." The dead in question are the "dead in Christ," namely, those who in this life belonged to, trusted in, and died committed to Christ.

Galatians

It is a very angry Paul who writes this letter to the Galatians. He goes so far as to call them "stupid Galatians" (3:1). He believes his apostolic authority has been undermined and hence insists that it derives from

Jesus and the Father "who raised him from the dead" (1:1). Clearly Paul feels hurt. This hurt stems from the Jewish Christian missionaries who taught Paul's Galatian converts that, to be right with God (justification), they had to accept circumcision and do the works of the Jewish law. Paul responds that those who have been incorporated into Christ are Abraham's descendants. As a result, they do not have to perform the works of the Jewish law. It is not surprising, therefore, that Paul devotes relatively little direct attention to the issues of the afterlife. However, his teaching on incorporation into Christ has relevance for eternal life and resurrection.

In 3:27 Paul stresses the crucial role of baptism in the lives of Christians: "For all of you who were baptized into Christ have clothed yourselves with Christ." Paul understands baptism as a rite by which the candidate attains union with Christ. The preposition "into" underlines this initial movement of incorporation. Clothing oneself in Christ suggests that Christ envelops baptismal candidates like a garment. In 3:28 Paul concludes that ethnic (Jew or Greek), social (slave or free), and gender (male or female) differences become inconsequential because of incorporation into Christ. While such distinctions separate people from each other in the world, those incorporated into Christ "are all one in Christ Jesus" (3:28). (Paul does not say that these distinctions are abolished, only that, as regards Christian baptism, they are irrelevant.)

In 2:20 Paul declares that salvation is happening right now: "yet I live, no longer I, but Christ lives in me." Hence Paul is alive to God. In the previous verse Paul solemnly acknowledges that he has been crucified with Christ. By such association he lives on a much different level—he belongs to the sphere of Jesus. Though he continues his ordinary earthly existence, Christ lives in him. In more technical terms, Paul now enjoys a new principle of activity that influences his whole being. Jesus has become that principle of activity.

In 6:15 Paul speaks about incorporation into Christ with a different image: "For neither does circumcision mean anything, nor does uncircumcision, but only a new creation." To be incorporated into Christ is to be incorporated into a new creation (see 2 Cor 5:17). In this new creation all those barriers of race, social status, and gender no longer exist, for all are one in Christ. This new reshaping of human existence on the level of being derives from an energizing force that has the capacity to re-create life. Creation is thus an ongoing reality. The God who created in the beginning continues to do so. To put it in different terms, a creation only in the beginning is unworthy of God.

Obviously Paul does not address the issues of eternal life and resurrection in any straightforward manner in this letter. However, he does provide the building blocks for grasping these issues. Baptism into Christ is that rite whereby believers achieve union with Christ. As a result, all those obstacles that keep people apart are obliterated—all the baptized are one in Christ. Christ has become the new principle of activity that impacts believers' entire being. They are on a much higher, more personal level—they are alive in Jesus. They are also a new creation since God in Christ has reshaped their human existence. As Paul will further demonstrate, eternal life and resurrection go hand in glove with this new creation. The God who created in the beginning by overcoming chaos effects a new creation by overcoming death.

Philippians

This is one of Paul's "captivity" letters (the others are Ephesians, Colossians, and Philemon) that portray Paul as no longer a free person. In fact, he may face the distinct possibility of death. Despite such circumstances, Paul finds reason to rejoice: "my situation has turned out rather to advance the gospel" (1:12). This atmosphere of joy pervades much of the letter. As he shares in Jesus' sufferings, Paul perceives more intimately the power that the resurrection exercises in his life. Having experienced such pain, Paul challenges the Philippians to imitate him. As one reads this letter, it becomes all too evident that Paul cherishes a deep affection for this community that has aided him financially and otherwise on more than one occasion.

In 1:18-26 Paul discusses the question of the advantages and disadvantages of his absence from the Philippian community. He states this dilemma in no uncertain terms: "now as always, Christ will be magnified in my body, whether by life or by death" (1:20). (By "body" Paul understands his entire self.) Either way Paul can derive both hope and joy. God will be honored whether he lives and thus continues to preach the Gospel or whether he surrenders his life in death. This is indeed a dilemma—he candidly remarks that he does not know which option to choose. He expresses the advantage of death thus: "I long to depart this life and be with Christ, for that is far better" (1:23). Then he observes that to continue living would be a great gain for the Philippians as well as his other converts, both past and future.

As in 1 Thessalonians, the phrase "to be *with* Christ" surfaces again. Some scholars understand "depart" in this verse to mean release of the body from the soul, hence a disembodied intermediate state with reunion of body and soul at the second coming. However, the verb "to depart" is simply a euphemistic way of expressing death. In 1 Thessalonians Paul views being with the Lord (4:17) as taking place at the second coming. Now, given the possible expectation of death, Paul thinks of union with the Lord in an intermediate state, that is, after death but before the second coming. While Paul sees this companionship as a reward for his faithful service in proclaiming the Gospel, he provides no specifics about the conditions in the intermediate state.

In 3:5-6 Paul offers details about his Jewish heritage. He states that he is a member of "the tribe of Benjamin, a Hebrew of Hebrew parentage, in observance of the law a Pharisee" (3:6). He goes on to note that he regards all this as loss because of Christ (3:7). He then states his present goal: "to know him and the power of his resurrection" (3:10). For Paul, the God who raised Jesus from the dead is a God of power. In raising Jesus, the Father endowed him with the power of new life (Rom 1:4; 2 Cor 13:4). However, this power envisions not only Jesus but also humankind. This power conferred by the Father energizes believers so that they can share Jesus' experience and live in union with him. The energizing that Paul describes in Galatians 2:20 originates with the Father's raising of Jesus.

While Paul and other believers share in Jesus' energizing power, they still long for the consummation of union with him. In 3:11 Paul speaks about attaining the resurrection from the dead. Once more, "already" but "not yet" converge. Already endowed with the life stemming from Jesus' resurrection, believers have not yet achieved the final step, namely, resurrection from the dead.

Paul returns to this final step in 3:20-21. He declares that the citizenship of believers is to be found in heaven (3:20). While Paul accepts the notion that they are enrolled as heavenly citizens, he is implying that they have not made it yet—their homeland is actually elsewhere. They still "await a savior, the Lord Jesus Christ" (3:20). According to 3:21, when that time arrives, Jesus "will change our lowly body to conform with his glorified body." Paul announces that the lowly body (the whole person) will be changed by Jesus into a glorified body. Indeed Jesus is the very exemplar of this transformation process since bodies will be conformed to his. The power to effect such changes comes from his Father who so endowed him in raising him from the dead.

Briefly stated, in Philippians Paul would like to be *with* Christ but to continue living would benefit the community. The notion of union *with* Christ emerges again. Paul speaks about the power of Jesus' resurrection, a power conferred by the Father to be shared with believers. This is the power that actually energizes them. Yet they must still wait for the final consummation when Christ will transform their lowly bodies into heavenly ones conformed to his own glorified body. The same resurrection power will be at work.

I Corinthians

For Paul, the Christian community at Corinth is both troubled and troubling. In response to reports about divisions in the community, Paul writes 1 Corinthians. In this letter (as well as in 2 Corinthians) he reveals his uncanny ability to apply the Gospel message to ever-changing circumstances. In 1 Corinthians he deals with such issues as the importance of spiritual gifts (e.g., speaking in tongues), the freedom to eat food sacrificed to idols, the celebration of the Eucharist, and the general resurrection of the dead. It is this last item that sheds enormous light on Paul's conception of the afterlife. However, there is one other passage that touches on the relevance of the body for Christians.

In 6:12-20 Paul grapples with the problem of casual sex with a prostitute. For the Corinthians, the body is morally irrelevant because death finally does away with it. Sex, therefore, with a prostitute is lawful because it is only a "body" thing. Paul responds to this argument by appealing to Jesus' resurrection: "God raised the Lord and will also raise us by his power" (6:14). Hence the body must be meaningful in God's eyes. Although resurrection removed Jesus from this visible, tangible world, it is the Christian community that still makes him present: "Do you not know that your body is a temple of the holy Spirit . . . and that you are not your own?" (6:19). Christians continue the mission of Jesus in their bodies, that is, by their physical presence in the world. As in Philippians, the power of Jesus' resurrection is at work in them (6:14). Believers share the new vitality of the risen One and his Spirit: "But whoever is joined to the Lord becomes one spirit with him" (6:17).

In 1 Corinthians 15 Paul takes up the special issue of the general resurrection of the dead that some members of the community are denying. Given the moral irrelevance of the body, he seems to be addressing those Corinthian Christians who support the Hellenistic denial of resurrection in favor of immortality of the soul. However, Paul may also have in mind those who accept only a limited resurrection, that is, restoration to life but not transformation into a new life. After stating the Christian creed about the resurrection of Jesus in 15:1-11, Paul dismantles the efforts of his opponents and presents his own understanding of the issue.

In 15:12-19 Paul considers the consequences of the thesis that the dead are not raised. He speaks of the intimate bond between the resurrection of Jesus and the resurrection of believers. For Paul, the resurrection of Jesus is not an isolated event that affects only him. Rather, it has repercussions for all believers: "For if the dead are not raised, neither has Christ been raised, and if Christ has not been raised, your faith is vain and you are still in your sins" (15:16-17). To deny Jesus' resurrection, therefore, renders the Corinthians' faith and salvation empty. Moreover, those who have died have not merely fallen asleep; they have perished (15:18). Paul concludes this section by observing that without the risen One, the Corinthians are only to be pitied (15:19).

In 15:20-28 Paul draws out the implications of the belief that Jesus has indeed been raised. He speaks of Jesus as the "firstfruits" (15:20, 23). The image of firstfruits implies that some fruit has already been picked and eventually other fruit will follow. Thus Jesus' resurrection announces the eventual resurrection of those who belong to him. While this is clearly a message of hope, it also establishes the close link between Jesus and believers. It guarantees the full ingathering of the faithful at the second coming. Paul also draws a contrast between Adam who brought death and Jesus who brings life: "For just as in Adam all die, so too in Christ shall all be brought to life" (15:22). Paul then turns to the time when all those in Christ will be raised at the second coming. When the forces of evil are finally vanquished, Jesus will present the kingdom to his Father (15:24).

In 15:35-50 Paul discusses the character of the resurrected body of believers by relating it to the resurrected body of Jesus. Referring to plant life, Paul notes that the plant developing from the seed is the same reality but it has basically a different body. God determines the final shape of the plant body. However, given the similarity of many seeds, humans are incapable of knowing God's intention from the form of the seed body (15:36-38). In 15:42-44 Paul contrasts the resurrected body with the present body. While the present body is perishable, dishonorable, weak, and physical, the resurrected body is imperishable, glorious, powerful, and spiritual. All believers now possess this "glory" (15:40-41) only in an initial way. But they will enjoy it completely in their resurrected body.

When Paul uses the term "body," he is generally speaking of the whole human person in his or her concrete existence. Such a person does not *have* a body—such a person *is* a body. According to Paul, at the general resurrection one does not merely survive death or is reconstituted as before. Rather, like the risen One, one is transformed. In 15:44 Paul calls such a transformed person a "spiritual" body. Spiritual, however, does not mean immaterial. It implies that at the resurrection the Spirit animates one's bodily existence. The same Spirit that transformed Jesus in his resurrection will also transform believers. Such life beyond death is the complete reintegration of the one's entire person.

As in 1 Thessalonians 4, Paul deals in 1 Corinthians 15 with two categories: (1) those already dead, and (2) those who will survive to the second coming. These survivors do not "die" in the same way but their bodies must be transformed: "We will not all fall asleep, but we will all be changed" (15:51). While repeating the sound of the trumpet from 1 Thessalonians 4:16, Paul provides a different aspect of the second coming. On that occasion death, the personification of everything that prevents community with God, will be overcome. Sin, the world's perverted value system that manipulates humans by demanding blind obedience to the law, will also be vanquished. Quoting Hosea 13:14, Paul breaks out into a song of thanksgiving: "Death is swallowed up in victory. / Where, O death, is your victory? / Where, O death, is your sting?" (15:54-55).

Summary

The death and resurrection of Jesus provide the prism for Paul to speak of the afterlife. Eternal life, therefore, means to live in the company of the risen Lord, to be *with* him. Such life begins with the incorporation of believers into Christ whereby they become a new creation. This stems from the power conferred by the Father on Jesus in raising him from the dead that, in turn, enables him to grant a new form of life to believers. For Paul, Jesus is the firstfruits of the resurrection of the dead, a metaphor implying the full ingathering of those who accept Jesus in faith.

While believers enjoy resurrection life now, they enjoy this glory only in an initial way—at the resurrection of the dead they will enjoy it fully. In speaking of the resurrection body, Paul employs the analogy of plant life (the seed versus the mature plant). Through this image Paul teaches that the resurrected bodies of believers will be imperishable, glorious, powerful, and spiritual. Thus the resurrection of the dead means transformation, not mere survival or reconstitution to one's previous existence.

Reflections

Unlike Luke in Acts, Paul states that he actually saw the risen Lord. It is this overpowering vision that radically changes him. He now sees everything—afterlife, interpersonal relations, the world of nature, to name only a few—through the prism of Jesus' death and resurrection. Paul, therefore, speaks from the vantage point of the Damascus encounter. It shapes both his way of thinking and his way of acting. Though he accepted the resurrection of the dead as a dedicated Pharisee, he now perceives that event against the background of God's act of raising Jesus from the dead.

Paul is alive to God. He attests in Galatians 2:20 that it is no longer he who lives but it is Christ who lives in him. Paul is already leading a life grounded in the death and resurrection of Jesus. He enjoys a new principle of action that influences his whole person. He wants to know Jesus but also the power of his resurrection (Phil 3:10). The Father endowed the Son with that power so that Paul and all believers can share Jesus' experience and live in union with him.

The event of Easter Sunday has repercussions for all believers. First, Jesus brings about the resurrection of believers. To rephrase 1 Corinthians 15:16-17, since Jesus has been raised, the dead can also be raised. Second, Jesus is the model or exemplar of the resurrection body. In Philippians 3:21 he announces that Jesus will transform the lowly bodies of believers so that they can be conformed to his own glorified body. Third, anyone in Christ is a new creation (Gal 6:15; see 2 Cor 5:17). The effects of Jesus' resurrection impact believers here and now. The transformation has already begun.

CHAPTER SIX

Paul

Part II and Interpreters

Key Biblical Passages: Romans 1:1-7; 6:1-14; 8:1-39; 2 Corinthians 3:7–4:18; 5:1-10; Ephesians 1:15-23; 2:1-10; Colossians 1:15-23; 3:1-17

2 Corinthians

Having suffered a rebuff from one of the Corinthians during a visit after writing 1 Corinthians (see 2 Cor 2:5-11), Paul returns to Ephesus and writes a harsh letter to that community (see 2 Cor 2:1-4—this letter is no longer extant). However, he later receives word that the Corinthians have repented—a situation that prompts the writing of 2 Corinthians (probably a composite of two distinct letters: chaps. 1–9 and chaps. 10–13). In both letters Paul is clearly on the defensive. Unlike the orderliness of 1 Corinthians, 2 Corinthians reveals an impassioned Paul who does not mask his personal hurt regarding attacks on his apostolic authority. In 2 Corinthians 3–5 he reflects on ministry and mortality.

Since Paul's enemies in Corinth compared him unfavorably with Moses (the epitome of Hellenistic virtues), Paul proceeds to refute the comparison by turning to the account of the second giving of the law and the veiling of Moses' face in Exodus 34:27-35. In 3:7–4:6 he contrasts that event with the experience of Jesus and believers. According to Exodus 34:30, the glory of God that caused Moses' face to shine frightened the Israelites. Unfortunately Moses' veil that was originally intended to conceal God's glory has now become the means of keeping the Israelites from understanding Moses' message: "To this very day, in fact, whenever Moses is read, a veil lies over their hearts" (3:15).

In contrast, the one who accepts Jesus in faith gazes with unveiled face on the glory of the risen Lord. Moreover, such a person is now being transformed gradually by degrees of glory reflected on and from the face of Jesus: "All of us, gazing with unveiled face on the glory of the Lord, are being transformed into the same image from glory to glory" (3:18). All light and glory originate with God the Creator (4:6). As the likeness or image of the Creator (4:4), Jesus reflects that light and glory on the faces of all those who turn to him in faith. Hence Paul attests that believers are now being transformed by degrees into the image or likeness of Jesus. Once more, "already" and "not yet" meet. The transformation of believers has already begun. However, the completion of that process in the resurrection has not yet occurred.

In 4:7-18 Paul challenges the Corinthians to view his ministry in the light of Jesus' death and resurrection. In 4:7-12 he states that his sufferings in proclaiming the Gospel actually share in the death/dying of Jesus. Paradoxically, however, they manifest the life of Jesus in Paul's mortal flesh: "always carrying about in the body the dying of Jesus, so that the life of Jesus may also be manifested in our body" (4:10). In 4:14 Paul declares that the Father who raised Jesus "will raise us also with Jesus and place us with you in his presence." In 4:15-17 Paul talks about his outer self that people can see and his inner self that people cannot see. Paradoxically this inner self is being renewed day by day. Affliction, therefore, "is producing for us an eternal weight of glory beyond all comparison" (4:17). For Paul, resurrection life is already functioning in his body.

In this passage Paul approaches the resurrection in two ways. First, should he die before the second coming, God will raise him from the dead as he raised the Lord from the dead (4:14). Second, Paul acknowledges that the power of the resurrection is already at work in the sufferings he endures for the gospel (4:16-17). In other words, resurrection has already broken into his mortal flesh as he struggles with pain and hardship. This is the paradox: strength in weakness and life in death.

In 5:1-10 Paul again considers the resurrection body but this time from a more personal perspective. Here he wishes to show his readers how the power of the resurrection operates in the demanding life of an apostle. He speaks of his mortal body as a fragile earthly tent that can break down at any moment. If that tent collapses, "we have a building, a dwelling not made with hands, eternal in heaven" (5:1)—a reference to the resurrection body. He trusts that he will be clothed, that is, enjoy a resurrection body so that "what is mortal may be swallowed up by life" (5:4). He believes that God will effect this transformation because he has provided the Spirit as a pledge (5:5). The Spirit as pledge or guarantee is the first payment or installment that assures believers that God will indeed provide them with a resurrection body. While he is alive, Paul is away from the Lord. However, he longs to be with the Lord in the resurrection (5:6-8).

Resurrection life is already functioning in earthly life. The lives of believers are already being transformed gradually into the image and likeness of Jesus who is the image of God. Moreover, the power of the resurrection comes into view paradoxically in moments of hardship and affliction. Believers, while they are away from the Lord, still long to be *with* him in their resurrection bodies that are a building from God, eternal in heaven, in contrast to the fragile earthly tent. Hope for this encounter rests with the Spirit who serves as a pledge or guarantee of God's promise.

Romans

As Paul writes this letter, he finds himself toward the end of his missionary career in the eastern Mediterranean. He intends to bring a generous gift of money from the Gentile Christian churches to the Jewish Christian church in Jerusalem. After his visit to Rome, he plans on going to Spain. In view of this he seeks to introduce himself to the Roman Christians (both Jewish and Gentile) by providing this most cogent statement of his gospel. Although Paul treats many of the same concerns in Galatians, in Romans he is obviously much more controlled and hence less polemical. As in Galatians, he argues that being right with God (justification) rests on faith, not good works. His overall message is the gospel of God (1:1) that is nothing less than the power of God for salvation (1:16). With regard to the afterlife Paul states that believers who die with Christ in baptism will also live with him. The death and resurrection of Jesus thus impact both the present and future lives of believers.

Paul writes yet again about the power of Jesus' resurrection and its relationship to the resurrection of believers. In the very beginning of Romans he speaks of Jesus as "established as Son of God in power according to the spirit of holiness through resurrection from the dead" (1:4). The Father's act of raising Jesus from the dead endows Jesus with power to effect the resurrection of believers. In 6:4 Paul declares that Jesus was raised by the *glory* of the Father—a reference to divine power like the Exodus miracles (see Exod 14:18). As seen in 2 Corinthians 3:18, this power/glory transforms believers. In 8:29 Paul states that the purpose of God's election of believers is to conform them to the image of his Son. Thus they look like Jesus and become members of his family: "so that he might be the firstborn among many brothers" ("brothers" includes sisters). While Jesus enjoys a preeminent place in the family as the firstborn, believers still share the status of his sisters and brothers. The bond is so intimate that not even death and its anxieties can sever family members from the love of God in Christ (8:38-39).

Several times in Romans Paul heightens the family dimension of Jesus' resurrection by emphasizing its effect on believers. Thus Jesus "was handed over to death for *our* transgressions and was raised for *our* justification" (4:25; see 2 Cor 5:15). For Paul, the resurrection of Jesus implies both the beneficiaries of this act (believers) and his empowerment from the Father to bring about their resurrection as family members.

In 6:1-14 Paul discusses the effects of Christian baptism and its connection to Jesus' death and resurrection. In baptism believers are introduced into the very act of Jesus' dying (6:3). In 6:4 Paul widens the perspective by including Jesus' burial and resurrection as well as his death: "We were indeed buried with him through baptism into death, so that, just as Christ was raised from the dead by the glory of the Father, we too might live in newness of life." Through baptism believers are identified with the glorified Lord and destined to be with him. (However, while believers are crucified with Christ, die with him, and are buried with him, they are not raised with him—something that Paul's interpreters will change.)

While Jesus, according to Paul, effects the resurrection of believers through the power conferred by God, he is also the exemplar or model of the resurrection: "we shall also be united with him [literally, grown together with him] in the resurrection" (6:5). Hence believers already share in Jesus' risen life. However, this is not the definitive final form of new life that will occur in the end: "If, then, we have died with Christ, we believe that we shall also live with him" (6:8).

In Romans 8 Paul analyzes life in the Spirit. He speaks once more of the "already" but "not yet." While believers already dwell in Christ through his Spirit, God "who raised Jesus from the dead will give life to your mortal bodies also, through his Spirit that dwells in you" (8:11).

This life-giving Spirit will complete believers' baptism in the resurrection on the last day. In 8:17 Paul expresses this point by referring to believers as coheirs with Christ, adding, "if only we suffer with him, so that we may also be glorified with him." By sharing in the sufferings of Jesus, believers will share totally in his risen glory in the overwhelming presence of the Father.

In 8:18-25 Paul introduces the notion of the transformation of the whole created world. Simply put, the end time is like the beginning. In both 1 Corinthians 15 and Romans 5 Paul contrasts Adam with Christ. Owing to the fall Adam became subject to death and was alienated from nature and the animal world. With Christ's death and resurrection a new creation has emerged (see 2 Cor 5:17). In this new creation the world Adam knew before the fall is reconstituted thanks to the life-giving Spirit of God. The creation of new beings in Christ involves the whole cosmos: "in hope that creation itself would be set free from slavery to corruption and share in the glorious freedom of the children of God" (8:20-21). While there is a close link between the transformation of the material world and the resurrection on the last day, the process of believers integrating themselves into this new order must take place now. Since resurrected life has already begun for believers, they are called to this task of integration at the present moment. To that extent ecology and hope of the resurrection are hardly odd bedfellows. While believers who possess the firstfruits of the Spirit groan inwardly (8:23), they are presently challenged to combine hope for the end time with efforts on behalf of the environment.

Succinctly put, Paul focuses in this letter on the intimate bond between the dead and risen Jesus and believers. They are conformed to him and become members of his family. Jesus' actions in both his death and resurrection envision family members as his beneficiaries. Through baptism they die and are buried with Christ. They are thus identified with him and destined to be with him—an event that will come to completion in the resurrection on the last day. Prior to that occurrence, believers must see themselves as contributing to the transformation of the material world—a challenge that is ongoing. Thus the resurrection on the last day is bound up with the task of integrating themselves at the present moment into this new order.

Colossians

Probably written by a disciple of Paul in the eighties, this "captivity" letter develops the theology of the author's mentor. While in

1 Corinthians 12:27 the Christian community is the Body of Christ, in Colossians Jesus has become the head of the Body that is the church (1:18). Advancing Paul's theology of reconciliation (2 Cor 5:18-20), this letter presents Christ as the one in whom divine fullness dwells so that God chooses to reconcile all things through him (1:19-20). With regard to the afterlife, the author opts to emphasize the hope and salvation already possessed by believers rather than the imminence of the second coming.

In the opening chapter the author links creation in the beginning to the new creation of life in the death and resurrection of Jesus: "He is the image of the invisible God, / the firstborn of all creation. / . . . He is the beginning, the firstborn from the dead, / that in all things he himself might be preeminent" (1:15, 18). Since he is the firstborn from the dead, he is also the firstborn of all creation. While Paul speaks of Jesus as "the firstfruits of those who have fallen asleep" (1 Cor 15:20), the author of Colossians prefers the expression "the firstborn from the dead" (1:18). Through his resurrection from the dead Jesus has inaugurated the final times. As the firstborn, he is necessarily joined to his extended family.

In Romans 6 Paul understands baptism as that rite in which believers are crucified with Christ, die with him, and are buried with him but are not raised with him. The author of Colossians advances his master's theology by including being raised with Jesus: "You were buried with him in baptism, in which you were also raised with him through faith in the power of God, who raised him from the dead" (2:12; see 3:1). Hence the resurrection of believers has already happened in baptism. The author does not call what lies ahead the resurrection of the dead. Rather, the future involves the revelation of the life already begun in baptism but still hidden in God (3:3): "When Christ your life appears, then you too will appear with him in glory" (3:4). The glory awaiting believers in the end is nothing less than the glory of the risen Lord. They will reach this fulfillment *with* Christ.

For the author of Colossians, believers already have one foot in heaven since they have been raised with Christ in baptism. The author complements this view by employing the firstborn from the dead metaphor for Jesus. At the same time the author cautiously reminds his readers that the end time, the time of revelation, still lies in the future. Having been raised with Christ, they must put to death whatever is of earth (3:5-11). Having been raised with him, they must also clothe themselves with a new way of life (3:12-17).

Ephesians

Writing under Paul's name in the nineties, the author of Ephesians composes a kind of circular letter to the Gentile Christians in Asia Minor (modern western Turkey). The tone of the letter suggests that the general audience did not know Paul in the flesh. He focuses on their status in Christ and heartily encourages them to live accordingly. He reminds them that they have benefited from his struggles for them and should, therefore, avoid any form of complacency. With regard to the afterlife Ephesians touches upon believers' present participation in the glory of the risen Lord, putting less emphasis on the resurrection on the last day.

In the thanksgiving (1:17) the author prays in the following way: "that the God of our Lord Jesus Christ, the Father of glory, may give you a spirit of wisdom and revelation resulting in knowledge of him." As seen in Romans 6:4, it is the Father's glory/power that raises Jesus from the dead—an action that results in newness of life for believers, an effect often associated with the role of the Spirit. A few verses later in this thanksgiving (1:20) the author states that God raised Jesus from the dead and seated him at his right hand in the heavenly places, thereby combining resurrection and ascension. In 2:4-6 he also writes, "But God . . . brought us to life with Christ . . . and seated us with him in the heavens in Christ Jesus." As Christ was raised, so believers are raised with him. As God made Christ to sit at his right hand, so believers sit with him. As a result, they clearly enjoy solidarity with Christ and possess at present a status of exaltation.

In 2:7, however, the author tempers this outlook somewhat in that the manifestation of salvation stretches out into the future: "that in the ages to come he might show the immeasurable riches of his grace in his kindness toward us in Christ Jesus." While believers already experience an exalted state, only the future will disclose its final implications, revealing to all God's superabundant grace. Hence the consummation will occur only in the final ages. Although presently sharing in Christ's resurrection and ascension, they must still lead a life worthy of their calling.

Summary

Paul states that one who accepts Jesus in faith looks with unveiled face on the glory of the risen One. Such a person is undergoing a gradual transformation through the glory reflected on and from the face of Jesus. However, it is still a matter of "already" but "not yet."

While the transformation process has already started, the completion of that process has not yet taken place.

In speaking of the resurrection body of believers, Paul uses another analogy in addition to that of plant life in 1 Corinthians 15. In 2 Corinthians 5 he employs the image of a tent versus a building. While the mortal body is a fragile earthly tent that can collapse at any moment, at the resurrection believers will be like a building that is God's handiwork. Paul asserts that believers will be clothed, that is, enjoy a resurrection body owing to the work of the Spirit. This Spirit is the pledge or guarantee that God will effect the transformation process.

Paul emphasizes the link between baptism and the death and resurrection of Jesus. Through baptism believers are crucified with Jesus, die with him, and are buried with him. However, they are not raised with him. Nonetheless Christians are thereby identified with Christ and destined to be *with* him. Moreover, Jesus is the exemplar of the resurrection—believers will be united with him in a resurrection like him. In that resurrection the Spirit plays a crucial role, completing the work begun in baptism. Paul also makes the point that the life-giving rite of baptism relates believers to the whole created world. As beneficiaries of the firstfruits of the Spirit, they must impact the material world so that its renewal will mean the return to the world of Adam before the fall.

The interpreters of Paul develop the theology of their mentor. In Colossians the author links creation in the beginning to the new creation of life in the death and resurrection of Jesus. As the firstborn from the dead, Jesus has inaugurated the final times. As the firstborn, he is also connected to his extended family. The writer expands Paul's thought by observing that in baptism believers are also raised from the dead with Jesus. Not focusing on the resurrection of the dead as such, this author holds that the future will involve the revelation of the life already begun in baptism but still hidden with Christ in God. The author of Ephesians also teaches that believers are raised from the dead with Christ in baptism. However, he adds that they are already seated with him in the heavenly places. Nevertheless, the consummation of that exalted state will come only in the final ages. As in Colossians, believers must continue to lead lives worthy of such a state.

Reflections

Jesus is the source of the Christian hope of heaven and the afterlife. He is also the firstborn among many sisters and brothers. Not even death with its attendant anxieties can separate family members from God's love in Christ. He is also the firstborn from the dead (Col 1:18). Through his resurrection Jesus has initiated the final times. As firstborn from the dead, he is forever linked to his extended family. Ultimately Christian hope does not reside in plans and programs or human inventions and policies. Rather Christian hope, and here hope of heaven, resides in a person, namely, Jesus, "who was handed over for our transgressions and was raised for our justification" (Rom 4:25).

Paul emphasizes the role of the Spirit in Romans 8. It is through the Spirit that God will effect the resurrection of the mortal bodies of believers. This life-giving Spirit will thus bring to completion what began with the rite of baptism. In the time between baptism and resurrection on the last day believers must lead authentic lives by following the lead of the Spirit. Genuine peace will be the end result of such endeavors.

Paul also sees a vital link between the transformation of the material world and resurrection on the last day. Since the resurrection process has already begun in baptism, believers are challenged to see this world from the vantage point of Jesus' resurrection. They must respect this fragile world by caring for its precious resources. Resurrection faith and ecology thus go hand in hand. To protect the environment is to prepare for the final transformation of this world and human existence on the last day.

CHAPTER SEVEN

The Letter to the Hebrews

Key Biblical Passages: Hebrews 2:10-18; 3:1-19; 4:1-16; 5:7-10; 9:11-28; 10:19-39; 12:14-29

Introduction

For this piece of New Testament literature, the title "letter" is misleading, although the conclusion of Hebrews (13:20-25) follows epistolary style. It is, rather, a sermon or homily elegantly composed by a first-rate theologian to address a situation among a group of Roman Christians. Written sometime between 75 and 90 AD, it focuses on Christians who have a great nostalgia for their Israelite heritage and who yearn for the return of the Levitical cult after the destruction of the Jerusalem temple in 70 AD. In response the author forcefully asserts that Jesus has rendered obsolete all sacrifices, the Levitical priesthood, and an earthly holy of holies. To this end he constructs the imagery of Jesus as a high priest whose sacrifice on Calvary and intercession in heaven are decidedly more effective than the cult in any sanctuary: "When he speaks of a 'new' covenant (Jer 31:31), he [God] declares the first one obsolete. And what has become obsolete and has grown old is close to disappearing" (8:13).

While the Gospel of John interprets Jesus' death on the cross as his exaltation and the bestowal of the Spirit on the community, Hebrews understands the scene on Calvary in terms of the Day of Atonement (Yom Kippur). Every year and only on its occasion could the Jewish high priest enter the holy of holies to make atonement for all the sins of the people of Israel (Lev 16). By contrast the death of Jesus, a high priest according to the order of Melchizedek, brings about forgiveness of sins once and for all. Jesus thereby fulfills what the Day of Atonement prefigured. By means of his self-giving Jesus enters into the heavenly sanctuary. Referring to the tent or tabernacle during Israel's forty-year wandering in the wilderness, the author maintains that the only true tabernacle is now in heaven.

With regard to the afterlife Hebrews does not discuss the makeup of the resurrection body after the manner of Paul in 1 Corinthians 15. However, like Paul, he firmly believes in the second coming of Jesus, acknowledging it to be the final phase of God's plan of salvation. What emerges with great clarity is the tension between the "already" but "not yet." While believers already enjoy the benefits of heaven, they have not yet attained their final goal—they must continue to uphold their confession of faith in the present. The imagery used in Hebrews to describe heaven reflects the contrast between the eternal, heavenly world and the transient, earthly one.

Roles of Jesus

The author provides a useful clue to the relationship between Jesus and believers when he calls the latter "partners of Christ" (3:14; see 3:1). This partnership results from the confidence that believers have to speak openly and honestly with God—hence a form of friendship. In support of this partnership, the author emphasizes the humanity of Jesus, a reality that establishes an intimate, vital bond between him and his followers. For example, Jesus can sympathize with human weaknesses because he "has similarly been tested in every way, yet without sin" (4:15). In addition, in the very face of death Jesus did not hesitate to appeal to his Father with loud cries and tears (5:7).

Perfected through such suffering, Jesus has become the source of salvation for others (5:9) and can thus bring family members to glory. The author of Hebrews speaks of Jesus as the trailblazer ("leader" in the NABRE translation) in this enterprise: God "should make the leader to their salvation perfect through suffering" (2:10; see Acts 3:15; 5:31). As trailblazer, he is the one who opens up the way for others. His suffering and death impact not only his own status but also that of others. Having passed through the heavens (4:14), Jesus has entered the heavenly sanctuary "on our behalf as forerunner" (6:20). Similar to the trailblazer imagery, "forerunner" conjures up the role of Jesus in running ahead and thus creating a path into the heavenly sanctuary for his followers. In 12:2 the author again employs the term "trailblazer" ("leader") and couples it with "perfecter of faith." As believers run their race, they fix their gaze on Jesus, who through the cross has made their glorification possible. To sum up, the life of believers on earth is a journey toward their home in heaven that Jesus has blazed for them.

Images of Heaven

Against the background of the Day of Atonement Jesus enters the holy of holies by his death. This true holy of holies is nothing less than the heavenly sanctuary: "he entered once and for all into the sanctuary, not with the blood of goats and calves, but with his own blood, thus obtaining eternal redemption" (9:12). By this means the author of Hebrews reinterprets the Old Testament's understanding of obtaining access to God by replacing it with Jesus and positioning sacred space not in the earthly sanctuary but in the heavenly one, namely, the presence of God. Briefly stated, real sacred space is heaven, not earth. "For Christ did not enter into a sanctuary made by human hands, a copy of the true one, but heaven itself, that he might now appear before God on our behalf" (9:24). The death of Jesus, therefore, is nothing less than the entrance of the true high priest into the heavenly sanctuary. Since Jesus' death is a cultic act, heaven is understandably a cultic place. The author of Hebrews thus constructs heaven as a sanctuary sanctified by Jesus' blood where the one great sacrifice continues. Heaven constantly evokes the memory of his self-giving in crucifixion. Believers are empowered to have access to this sacred space by sharing in Jesus' sacrificial death.

The image of heaven as a city plays a conspicuous role in Hebrews. For the author, the reality of earth differs radically from that of heaven. Believers on earth have no lasting city but must seek one in heaven (13:14). In 12:22 the author confidently announces to his readers, "No, you have approached Mount Zion and the city of the living God, the heavenly Jerusalem." Mount Zion was the stronghold that King David established as his capital. In the Psalms it is frequently recognized as God's dwelling place. The earthly Mount Zion has now given way to the heavenly Jerusalem, the ultimate quest of the addressees in Hebrews. As the city of the living God, heaven surpasses all earthly dwelling places.

Speaking of such biblical characters as Abraham and Sarah, the author remarks that they died in faith as only strangers and foreigners on earth: "they desire a better homeland, a heavenly one" (11:16). In this context heaven connotes the homeland of the searchers. Believers share the company of Abraham and his once barren wife Sarah. With them they can receive their promised inheritance (9:15). It should also be noted that believers already possess an "unshakable kingdom" (12:28).

Heaven and Sabbath Rest

In Hebrews 3–4 the author employs the term "rest" no less than nine times, a number that suggests its importance. In 3:8 he quotes Psalm 95, in which Israel tests God in the wilderness. Angered by the resistance of the Israelites, God swears, "They will not enter into my rest" (3:11). Unfortunately the meaning of "rest" is elusive. Some take it in a geographical sense, for example, Numbers 14:30, where God states that the wilderness generation (with the exception of Joshua and Caleb) will not enter the Promised Land. Hence that land is the place of rest. However, it appears more likely that "rest" should be taken as a state. As such, it can reflect three periods of time: (1) the past (God's Sabbath rest after completing creation); (2) the present (the actual possession of this state by the audience of Hebrews); and (3) the future (the goal or end of the believers' journey in faith).

The model of rest for believers is God's work stoppage following the six days of creation: "And God rested on the seventh day from all his works" (4:4). The Sabbath rest calls forth images of peace, contentment, and ease. For the author, believers already enjoy such rest: "For we who believed enter into that rest" (4:3). However, they have not fully entered into that rest—it is still future-oriented. "Therefore, a sabbath rest still remains for the people of God. And whoever enters into God's rest, rests from his own works as God did from his" (4:9-10). The warning from the rebellion of the wilderness generation serves a timely purpose—the audience of Hebrews must not fail through disobedience.

The view of the afterlife as entrance into a Sabbath rest involves more than the cessation from further work. It evokes the sense of peace and contentment that follows upon the work stoppage. It also conveys the sense of community. The believers are invited to join God in the celebration of the seventh day. The object of their arduous pilgrimage of faith is the enjoyment of the satisfaction that comes from following Jesus, their trailblazer and advance runner. "Rest in peace" certainly applies here.

The Challenge of the Tension of "Already" but "Not Yet"

For the author, no doubt exists that the end time has been inaugurated. Right at the very start of this sermon he marks a clear contrast between the past and the present. Long ages ago God spoke to the ancestors of the addressees by means of the prophets. However, "in these last days he spoke to us through a son" (1:2). In 6:4 tasting the heavenly gift is parallel with sharing in the Holy Spirit and tasting "the good word of God and the powers of the age to come" (6:5). In advance Jesus has sanctified them by his once and for all self-offering (10:14). The place of their Sabbath rest is a present reality since they have already arrived in "the heavenly Jerusalem" (12:22) and are now receiving an "unshakable kingdom" (12:28).

At the same time the specter of "not yet" hangs over the heads of the audience. A Sabbath rest still remains for the people of God (4:9). The author makes his audience all too aware of Jesus' second coming when God will conclude the plan of salvation: "Christ . . . will appear a second time, not to take away sin but to bring salvation to those who eagerly await him" (9:28). Quoting Habakkuk 2:3, the author announces, "he who is to come shall come; he shall not delay" (10:37).

These addressees already have one foot in the heavenly sanctuary but have not yet completed their journey. Their challenge consists in living in the present but keeping one eye focused on the future. To make this point, Hebrews reinterprets Psalm 95, insisting on the urgency of "today" by remaining loyal to God (3:13). Such present activity includes holding fast to their confession of faith (4:14), approaching God in confidence (10:19), and pursuing peace within their community (12:14). Briefly stated, the challenge faced by the addressees is the following: while sharing now in the invisible benefits of heaven, believers must realize that such sharing will be definitive only when they appear with Jesus in the eternal presence of the Father.

Summary

Hebrews presents Jesus as a high priest whose death on Calvary fulfills what the Day of Atonement prefigured. By means of this self-giving, Jesus is exalted by entering the heavenly sanctuary. However, Jesus' exaltation does not separate him from his followers. By underlining Jesus' humanity, the author establishes a very intimate bond between the exalted One and believers. Jesus relates to them as pioneer/trailblazer and forerunner.

A first image of heaven is the sanctuary sanctified by Jesus' blood where the one great sacrifice continues. In contrast to the lack of a lasting city on earth, Hebrews uses a second image, namely, that of a permanent city of the living God as well as that of the heavenly Jerusalem.

Heaven is also presented as the state of the Sabbath rest. Drawing from God's rest on the seventh day after creation (the past), the image also applies to the present (a state possessed by the addressees) and the future (the actual goal of believers). The image conjures up an atmosphere of peace and contentment. It also implies a community dimension since believers are invited to enter into God's rest.

Finally the tension between "already" but "not yet" surfaces yet again. With the inauguration of the final times believers already experience the powers of the age to come and have already arrived in the heavenly Jerusalem. However, the second coming has not yet taken place and a Sabbath rest still remains. The challenge for believers is to live in the present but to keep one eye focused on the future. In the meantime the addressees must continue to demonstrate their obedience and loyalty.

Reflections

While the Gospel of John views the death of Jesus as his exaltation, the author of Hebrews offers a different twist. Jesus' death is nothing less than a cultic act—it involves liturgy. Specifically Good Friday fulfills the intent of the Jewish feast of the Day of Atonement. By his sacrificial death Jesus, a high priest, enters the heavenly sanctuary. Since his death is cultic, heaven is also necessarily cultic. Believers gain access to this cultic setting by sharing in Jesus' sacrificial death. All this implies that they attain genuine sacred space only in heaven. While earthly sacred space is by definition transient, heavenly sacred space is alone eternal.

Hebrews teases one's imagination by conceiving of heaven as a city. Just as earthly sacred space is transient, so also the earthly city. The earthly Mount Zion must concede pride of place to the heavenly Jerusalem. Hebrews pictures believers as wayfarers, namely, those on a journey to their homeland. On earth believers share the company of Abraham and Sarah in that they are also strangers and foreigners. They too are looking for the better heavenly country. There they will receive their promised eternal inheritance.

One might think that such ethereal language tends to separate Jesus, a high priest in the heavenly sanctuary, from believers/wayfarers. However, Hebrews precludes such a notion by emphasizing the humanity of Jesus in both his temptations and his painful appeals to the Father for help. In Hebrews, as in Acts, Jesus acts as the pioneer/ trailblazer in opening up the way to the heavenly sanctuary. He also functions as their forerunner by dashing ahead and preparing their entrance into the heavenly Jerusalem. Hebrews introduces believers as partners of Christ—they are friends who can address Jesus openly and honestly as they make their way heavenwards.

As a complement to the cultic setting, the author presents the notion of a Sabbath rest. Recalling the divine work stoppage after six days of creation, believers focus on the goal of their journey of faith. Heaven thus represents more than the cessation of labor. It conjures up images of peace, contentment, and ease. By celebrating the weekly Sabbath rest, believers enter into the whole rhythm of creation, demonstrating that the end time in the heavenly sanctuary will be like the beginning in creation.

CHAPTER EIGHT

The Book of Revelation

Key Biblical Passages: Revelation 1:1-8; 4:1-11; 5:1-14; 6:1-17; 12:1-18; 13:1-18; 19:1-10; 20:1-15; 21:1-27; 22:1-5

Introduction

The book of Revelation, also known as the Apocalypse of John, does not fit neatly into one clearly defined literary genre. Like Daniel 7–12, it is apocalyptic, namely, a revelatory literature set in a narrative framework in which an otherworldly being discloses something transcendent to a human. Thus Jesus communicates God's message to an angel who speaks to John about the ultimate victory over evil. As an apocalyptic work, this book abounds in symbolism. For example, the dragon personifies the evil empire of Rome. Bearing such names as the devil, the serpent, and Satan, the dragon threatens the author's audience. At the same time Revelation is also prophecy, exhorting believers to repentance and holding out the chance for forgiveness: "Blessed is the one who reads aloud and blessed are those who listen to this prophetic message and heed what is written in it" (1:3). Finally Revelation is also a letter written to seven Christian communities in the Roman province of Asia (western Turkey). In sum, the book of Revelation is a prophetic-apocalyptic composition in the form of a letter to particular communities. Proper interpretation of Revelation does not entail decoding its data to extract predictions about the end of the world. To understand its message, the interpreter, in addition to appreciating the different literary components, must situate this unique biblical work in its proper setting.

Written by an unknown Christian prophet during the reign of the Roman emperor Domitian (81–96 AD), Revelation unfolds a dualistic world of black and white, evil and good—there is no middle ground. Rome with its imperial cult (Caesar is divine, not God) diametrically opposes the message of Jesus, especially as manifested in his crucifixion. It is not a question necessarily of active persecution of Christians. Rather, the danger faced by Christians is the dominant social forces of Rome at work in the Christian communities addressed. The author of Revelation (hereafter John) will tolerate no sort of accommodation with Roman society. Although Paul in Romans 13:1-3 speaks of not resisting the civil authorities and the author of 1 Timothy 2:2 recommends praying for such authorities, John rules out any and all compromises. Believers must resist by witness and martyrdom if required, not by violence. For example, in 18:4 a heavenly voice cries out, "Depart from her [Babylon = Rome], my people, / so as not to take part in her sins." Not surprisingly martyrdom plays a conspicuous role in this work.

With regard to the afterlife, John seeks to open the minds of his audience to the reality beyond the present visible world. To achieve this, John expands their minds by focusing on the heavenly realm and the prospects of the end time. From chapter 4 on, John finds himself in heaven, where he is privy to heavenly visions and auditions that impact his earthly Christian audience. From this perspective he will disclose the new heaven and the new earth (21:1) as well as the new Jerusalem, the city of God (21:9–22:5). While John does not discuss the resurrection body after the manner of Paul, he does consider two resurrections that relate to the struggle of good versus evil.

Images of Jesus

Like Colossians 1:18, Jesus is the firstborn of the dead (1:5). In 1:18 Jesus announces, "Once I was dead, but now I am alive forever and ever." Elsewhere John speaks about Jesus as "caught up to God and his throne" (12:5), a reference to his death and resurrection. Employing messianic imagery, John describes him as the lion of the tribe of Judah, the root of David (5:5). Similarly Jesus holds the key of David (3:7), demonstrating complete authority over heaven and earth. In 1:18 he possesses the keys of death and the netherworld—through his death and resurrection he has conquered the realm of death. (See also the combination of keys and the netherworld in Jesus' commissioning of Peter in Matthew 16:18-19.)

John also applies to Jesus what he applies to God. In 1:8 and 21:6 God receives the following titles: "the Alpha and the Omega; "the one who is and who was and who is to come"; and "the beginning and the end."

Likewise in 1:17 and 22:13 Jesus is acknowledged as "the first and the last," "the Alpha and the Omega," and "the beginning and the end." By such titles John constructs a very intimate relationship between God and Jesus. As in the Gospel of John, God reveals himself completely to Jesus. For John, God is present in Jesus. Indeed, he is God's very presence as he makes his way among the churches. Moreover, in contrast to the Roman emperor, only Jesus deserves to be called "Lord of lords and king of kings" (17:14; 19:16).

The definitive title for Jesus in this work is undoubtedly the Lamb. However, John qualifies this title by speaking of the Lamb that was slain: "Then I saw . . . a Lamb that seemed to have been slain" (5:6). In the opening chapter of his work John refers to Jesus as the one "who loves us and has freed us from our sins by his blood" (1:5). Fittingly the four living creatures and the twenty-four elders fall before the Lamb, singing, "Worthy are you to receive the scroll and break open its seals, for you were slain and with your blood you purchased for God those from every tribe and tongue, people and nation" (5:9). This metaphor of the slain Lamb, therefore, identifies Jesus as Messiah against the background of his victory on Calvary. In turn, the metaphor calls upon John's audience to follow the Lamb by faithful witness, even to the point of death, if necessary.

Just as John has constructed a very intimate relationship between God and Jesus, he does the same for the bond between Jesus and believers. In 12:10, in the aftermath of Michael's victory over the great dragon, a heavenly voice proclaims, "For the accuser [Satan] of our brothers [the term includes sisters] is cast out." In 14:13 another heavenly voice announces the blessedness of those faithful ones who die in the Lord, that is, sharing not only his death but implicitly at least his resurrection as well. In 7:17 one of the elders tells John in the vision of the anticipated victory of the martyrs that the Lamb "will shepherd them and lead them to springs of life-giving water." While Paul in 1 Corinthians 15:20, 23 speaks of Jesus as the firstfruits of the dead, John now characterizes the loyal companions of the Lamb, the redeemed, as the firstfruits of his harvest of salvation (14:4). In 19:9 an angel informs John that the righteous witnesses are invited to the marriage feast of the Lamb, a scene that expresses the intimacy and sense of community between the Lamb and his guests.

In his opening address John designates the recipients as a kingdom and priests (1:6). In so doing, he borrows from Exodus 19:6, where God designates the people of Israel at Sinai as a kingdom of priests. Following

Michael's victory over the dragon, a heavenly voice describes the successful outcome of the martyrs' witness: "They conquered him [Satan] by the blood of the Lamb / and by the word of their testimony; / love for life did not deter them from death" (12:11). Jesus' victory on the cross is their victory as well. In addressing the Christian community at Pergamum John writes that the loyal victors will receive a new name (2:17). This new name suggests the new life given by Jesus.

Liturgy

Worship plays a very large role in Revelation. This is hardly surprising since the work is clearly earmarked for public reading in a liturgy (1:3). Given the priestly status of the recipients (1:6), one naturally expects that these heavenly liturgies will serve a practical purpose, namely, the promotion of worship of God alone, not the Roman emperor. To this end, on two occasions the angel accompanying John must instruct him not to worship angels: "I am a fellow servant of yours . . . Worship God" (19:10; see 22:9). For John, a truly Christian life makes liturgy a central feature. In addition, worship of God looks forward to the consummation in the new heaven and the new earth.

The heavenly liturgy in Revelation 4–5 exemplifies the scope and relevance of divine worship. In 4:2 God is seated on a heavenly throne. The four living creatures acknowledge the uniqueness and apartness of the throne's occupant as they ceaselessly sing, "Holy, holy, holy is the Lord God almighty, / who was, and who is, and who is to come" (4:8). Following this, the twenty-four elders address God as the Creator who alone deserves "glory and honor and power" (4:11). As the scene continues, the Lamb receives the scroll from the One seated on the throne (5:7). After two hymns in honor of the Lamb, John introduces a third hymn in honor of both God and the Lamb: "To the one who sits on the throne and to the Lamb be blessing and honor, glory and might, forever and ever" (5:13). While humans cannot describe God as he actually is, they can and indeed must worship God. Only through worship can one genuinely acknowledge the divine majesty and uniqueness.

This last passage does not limit worship to the heavenly sphere. In 5:13 John specifically observes that all creatures in heaven, on earth, and under the earth must break out into song, confessing the honor due to both God and the Lamb. Elsewhere the martyred dead call out to God (6:10) and God's people as a whole direct their prayers to the Lamb (5:8). Worship is not a task that falls to a privileged few. Rather, it is the task incumbent on all creatures in the presence of the Creator.

This orchestra of worshipers is composed of all who duly recognize their creaturely status. The book of Revelation will show that the afterlife continues the chorus of praise already begun in heaven and on earth.

"Already" but "Not Yet"

This tension, already discussed in other New Testament works, finds its way into Revelation. Authors very often use a military strategy to illustrate this impasse. In a war one can readily sense when the momentum has shifted to such an extent that one side has clearly won. However, the last battle is yet to be fought. While the martyrs already rest under the altar, they are nonetheless told to rest a little longer (6:9, 11). Their salvation will be final only when the faithful enter the city of God.

This tension appears in the titles applied to God. In 1:8 God offers this self-description: "the one who is and who was and *who is to come*." The four living creatures refer to God in precisely the same way (4:8). Hence final victory has not yet come. However, in 11:17 the twenty-four elders fall down in worship, declaring, "Lord God almighty, who are and who were." Similarly the angel of the waters in 16:5 employs the same expression. As a result, without any reference to a future coming, God's victory is now complete.

In 12:8-9 Michael triumphs over the great dragon in heaven so that the dragon and his angels are subsequently thrown down to earth. However, after the woman (the heavenly Israel) has successfully eluded the dragon (12:16), the dragon continues to make war on the rest of her children (12:14). Thereafter, a first beast (representing the Roman emperor) and a second beast (symbolizing the imperial cult) persist in harassing God's people (13:1, 11). While Michael has already defeated the dragon, the dragon together with the other two beasts demonstrates that the final battle has not yet been fought. The situation is not unlike that of the destruction of Babylon (Rome). In 18:2 an angel invested with great authority issues the proclamation that Babylon the great has already fallen. However, a mighty angel casts a great millstone into the sea, saying, "With such force *will* Babylon the great city *be thrown down*" (18:21). Obviously the tension is not resolved.

The Martyrs and the First Resurrection

When Jesus opens the fifth seal, John sees "underneath the altar the souls of those who had been slaughtered because of the witness they bore to the word of God" (6:9). These martyrs are believers who will suffer death in the persecution about to begin. In so doing, they will share the destiny of Jesus (see 1:9; 12:11). Their location under the altar is telling. According to Leviticus 4:7 the priest must pour the remainder of the blood of a bull (a sin offering) at the base of the altar of burnt offerings. In other words, John presents the martyrs as sacrificial victims. Located under the heavenly altar, they find themselves at rest in the presence of God. According to Leviticus 17:11, 14, life is believed to reside in the blood of both humans and animals. The word translated "souls" above (6:9) stands for life or self. Hence John does not dwell on any intermediate state of disembodied souls prior to the resurrection. Rather, he focuses on the selves of the Christian martyrs. Against the background of the priestly status of Christians, these martyrs, therefore, function as priests who sacrifice themselves on God's altar.

In 6:10 the martyrs cry aloud to God, asking how long it will take to judge their oppressors and avenge their blood. It is very significant that the martyrs entrust their vindication to God (see Rom 12:19). Although bellicose imagery abounds in Revelation, John maintains that Jesus has won the war against evil by his death on the cross. In this way the martyrs will also conquer. Through their death God will vindicate them by showing them that the cross represents the standard of victory. In this way the seemingly helpless martyrs are the winners and the forces of evil the losers. John teaches that to respond to violence with greater violence is only to continue the spiral of inhumanity that plagues God's creation.

In 6:11 the martyrs receive a white robe that symbolizes their victory and hence their vindication. However, they are instructed to hold out a little longer "until the number was filled of their fellow servants and brothers who were going to be killed as they had been." This exhortation does not mean that there is some predetermined number of victims. Instead, the death suffered by the martyrs brings the end time closer. Those still on earth must derive hope from the fate of the martyrs that through the same self-sacrifice they too will pass beyond death into their heavenly rest.

In 20:1-6 John discusses the first resurrection. Here an angel seizes the dragon/serpent/devil/Satan and throws him into the bottomless pit for a period of a thousand years (a symbolic number). Most likely the beheaded martyrs occupy thrones to pass judgment. John underlines their loyalty by mentioning "their witness to Jesus and for the word of God" (20:4). Next they "came to life and they reigned with Christ for a thousand years" (20:4). John observes that this is indeed a special resurrection in that it precedes the general resurrection of the dead (see 20:11-15) by a thousand years. (Only the book of Revelation speaks of two resurrections.) This symbolic period of time represents a temporary era of righteousness prior to the final consummation. Significantly the martyrs exercise their regal status by reigning with Christ. For John, resurrection means that the martyrs are *with* Jesus. Without speculating on the form of a resurrected body, John insists that their death for Jesus and his message results in sharing the company of the Lamb.

"The New Heaven and the New Earth"

In 21:1 John begins with the overwhelming statement that he sees "a new heaven and a new earth." Relying on the legacy of the Old Testament, he draws his inspiration from the book of Isaiah: "Lo, I am about to create new heavens and a new earth . . . For I create Jerusalem to be a joy . . . No longer shall the sound of weeping be heard there" (Isa 65:17-19; see 2 Pet 3:10). As John expands his vision, he presents the new creation as a transformation of the old in which God redeems the world from being out of joint with his plan of salvation. In 21:1 he notes that the sea is no more, that is, the primeval ocean, the symbol of utter chaos, retreats and finally disappears. Actually the sea is but one of seven elements that the Creator God tactfully removes. The remaining destructive elements are (1) death (21:4), (2) mourning (21:4), (3) crying (21:4), (4) pain (21:4), (5) anything accursed (22:3), and (6) night (22:5). John takes pains to point out the origin of this new creation, namely, "coming down out of heaven from God" (21:2). Adapting once again the language of Isaiah, John depicts the new Jerusalem as a bride adorned for her husband (see 21:2; see Isa 49:18; 61:10). This double image of the city and bride contrasts sharply with Babylon, the great whore in Revelation 17.

John stresses the dimension of community when he cites a loud voice from the throne: "Behold, God's dwelling is *with* the human race. He will dwell *with* them and they will be his people and God himself will always be *with* them" (21:3). The God of John's vision cannot stand aloof from his creation. This is not the unmoved mover of Greek philosophy but the passionate God who rewards the faithful with the gift of abiding presence. It is hardly surprising that John envisions this involved God as gently wiping away the tears from their eyes (21:4).

There are several other features of this transformation that merit attention. Water plays a crucial role since it symbolizes nothing less than life itself: "To the thirsty I will give a gift from the spring of life-giving water" (21:6). However, John also observes that this life-giving spring symbolizes divine generosity—it is a gift. Capturing the family dimension of the faithful, John remarks that they will inherit these things as God's daughters and sons (21:7). Finally in 21:8 all sin is banished and its perpetrators relegated to the fire- and sulfur-filled lake.

The end time is like the beginning. The attentive reader cannot help but notice the overtones of Genesis 1–2. God's radical transformation recalls the pristine state of the divine achievement in the first creation. Once again God has overcome the unruly waters of chaos and constructed a cosmos that reflects both divine workmanship and aesthetics. This is a world where humans interact with God as they carry out their mandate to maintain balance and harmony in all facets of the new heaven and the new earth. The intimate bond between humankind and cosmos cannot be overstated.

The New Jerusalem

In 21:9–22:5 the new heaven and the new earth provide the setting for the new Jerusalem. An angel promises to show John this bride, the wife of the Lamb (21:9). (In the Old Testament the relationship between God and the city is frequently described as a marriage.) Owing to its heavenly origin, the city basks in divine glory (21:11). Part of the construction plan calls for twelve foundation stones (21:14) that are actually the precious stones enumerated in 21:19-20. (See Tobit 13:16-17 that prophesies the rebuilding of Jerusalem with such precious stones.) Again John establishes a marked contrast to the jewels of pagan Babylon/Rome, that other city (17:4). John offers yet another contrast to the old Jerusalem and its central edifice, the temple. In this new Jerusalem the material temple has disappeared, giving way to its replacement, namely, God and the Lamb (21:22). Given the divine presence, the need for luminaries such as the sun and the moon has vanished since "the glory of God gave it light, and its lamp was the Lamb" (21:23).

Rounding out this magnificent vision, John chooses to combine Ezekiel's river of life flowing from the temple (Ezek 47:1-12) with the streams in paradise that irrigate the Garden of Eden (Gen 2:10-14): "On either side of the river grew the tree of life" (22:2). This tree of life recalls the luxuriant vegetation that results from Ezekiel's river of life (Ezek 47:12) as well as the tree of life in Eden (Gen 2:9; 3:22). Here as well, John forges the link between the beginning and the end time. However, the exuberance of water and accompanying vegetation soon give way to the central intent of Revelation, namely, worship. Although Moses was not permitted to see God's face, in this new age the intimacy and sense of community with God not only allow such vision but even seem to demand it. Appropriately the faithful witnesses will reign with God forever and ever (22:5). Such is the family gathering in the new Jerusalem.

Summary

As a prophetic-apocalyptic work in the form of a letter, Revelation seeks to encourage Christian communities in Asia Minor to remain faithful to the message of Jesus. Such fidelity means no accommodation to the dominant social forces of the Roman Empire. In fact, it may even require martyrdom. The model for such resistance is Jesus, especially under the title of the Lamb. His victory on the cross is designed to be their victory as well.

In light of the imperial cult, liturgy plays a conspicuous role in Revelation. Although Christians are tempted to worship Caesar as lord, they must persevere in acknowledging only God and the Lamb as Lord. Against the background of the connection between heaven and earth both spheres must break out in song, confessing the honor due to God and the Lamb.

As in other New Testament works, the tension between "already" and "not yet" also applies here. Even though Michael has already conquered the great dragon, the faithful remain subject to the attacks of his minions. This tension also holds true for the martyrs. While they rest in the presence of God in heaven, they will achieve final salvation only in the end. However, the end for these martyrs occurs in the first resurrection, that is, they enjoy a special resurrection prior to the general resurrection of the dead.

To bolster the faith and commitment of his audience, John envisions for them "a new heaven and a new earth" as well as a new Jerusalem. In both cases it is a question of radical transformation. Eternal bliss for the faithful consists in the fact that God will dwell with them and be *with* them. In this new Jerusalem the twelve foundation stones are precious stones that contrast sharply with the jewelry worn by that other city, Babylon/Rome. Here there is no temple because God and the Lamb replace the old edifice. References to the water of life and the tree of life recall the creation stories in Genesis 1–2. The end time, therefore, is like the beginning. In this new age the faithful witnesses will reign *with* their God.

Reflections

Whereas the Gospel of John sees Good Friday as Jesus' exaltation and Hebrews views it as the Day of Atonement, Revelation strikes a slightly different note by its use of the title "the Lamb." Revelation qualifies this title by adding "slain." By his blood this slaughtered Lamb has won salvation for all. Calvary thereby becomes the scene of his victory over the powers of evil, a victory on which believers pin their hopes of remaining faithful and thus reaching heaven. However, the cost of victory is high—it may require martyrdom.

Revelation speaks of just such martyrs in 6:9, as they occupy a place under the heavenly altar as sacrificial victims. Given the bellicose setting of this biblical book, the cry for revenge is not unexpected. The martyrs inquire how long it will take God to judge their oppressors and avenge their blood. Following the lead of the distraught petitioners in the psalms of lament, the martyrs entrust God with the task of vindication. By so doing, they will end up winners, not the forces of evil.

The heavenly liturgy abounds in expressions of praise for God and the Lamb. These doxologies, however, are not limited to the voices in heaven. Believers on earth must also join in this unceasing chorus of praise. In Revelation one naturally anticipates such a central role for liturgy since believers enjoy a priestly status. Moreover, in expressing this status, they recognize God's majesty not only on earth but also prepare themselves for this unceasing role in heaven. In refusing to worship the emperor, they announce their allegiance to God and the Lamb, the only worthy recipients of their homage.

While Revelation's depiction of the new heaven and the new earth underlines the sense of community by having God dwell *with* the faithful, it also draws attention to another aspect of heaven, namely, the removal of all destructive forces. Besides the absence of the sea, anything accursed, and night, the text also includes death, mourning, crying, and pain. For the original addressees threatened with the possibility of martyrdom, a world free of these disturbing realities is heaven indeed. But even without the threat of martyrdom, such a world must energize the human spirit where so many encounter death, mourning, crying, and pain. The gentle gesture of God wiping away the tears of his extended family continues to provide hope for a world all too weary of the forces of evil.

CHAPTER NINE

A Heavenly Agenda

Introduction

In light of the biblical affirmations of heaven, how should believers conduct themselves during their time on earth? In other words, what impact should the Old and New Testaments have on the way they lead their daily lives? What kind of heavenly agenda does the Bible set for those who accept this wealth of biblical tradition? While heaven is indeed a place, this agenda accentuates heaven more as a mode of life or state of being. Hence the precise location of heaven does not enter into this discussion.

Jesus as the Focus

One may rightly declare that Jesus is heaven. By his death and resurrection he has forever changed the face of death and the notion of the afterlife. The action of the Father in sending the Spirit to breathe transforming life into the dead body of Jesus affects all believers. The Gospel of John and the letters of Paul attest that followers of Jesus already enjoy to some degree his resurrection life. They have come to know, as Paul says, the power of his resurrection. In focusing on Jesus, believers acknowledge that Jesus not only brings about their resurrection but also that he represents the norm or standard of resurrected life. The bodily resurrection of believers necessarily follows upon God's raising of Jesus from the dead.

To borrow the language of Acts and Hebrews, Jesus has become the trailblazer. By his death and resurrection he opens up the way to the afterlife. As firstborn from the dead, he extends the hope of resurrection to his sisters and brothers. As firstfruits, he assures them of a bountiful harvest. At the same time the hour for the final resurrection of disciples has not yet struck. A significant item on the agenda must be the centrality of Jesus in their lives now.

Jesus is humanity as God intends humanity to be. He represents the fullness of what it means to be truly human. Humans, however, tend to extrapolate models for living from the ranks of fallen humanity. They resort, for example, to the worlds of Hollywood and professional sports to find their superheroes and guides for living life to the fullest. Paul sees such a tendency in his Corinthian community. He urges them, therefore, to refocus and realign their priorities in the proper order. In the selection process of the genuinely human he cautions, "Accept no substitutes—only Jesus will do!" While living resurrection life now, believers must relentlessly choose Jesus and eschew all others. If Jesus is indeed heaven, only those who follow him in the folly of the cross and the fullness of the empty tomb gain acceptance. To follow such an agenda is to know the power of his resurrection.

Community with God

The elusive preposition "with" reveals the community dimension of heaven. For example, in Revelation 21:3 God establishes his home among humans and dwells *with* them. God appears as the very center or goal of all human endeavors. The author of Psalms 42–43 offers a vivid description of this powerful drive toward community with God, although it does not involve an afterlife: "As the deer longs for streams of water, / so my soul longs for you, O God" (42:2). An animal thirst for God devours the psalmist's entire being ("soul"). Such a thirst captures to some extent the sense of community with God in heaven. In this case it is presence, not absence, that makes the heart grow fonder. Eternal life with God means much more than the continuation of life. A paradigm shift occurs as endless existence with God moves to the quality of life with God.

While the aspect of individual fulfillment occupies a proper place in the concept of heaven, it still remains inadequate. The heaven symbol is not in single file with sole emphasis on "me, myself, and I." Community with God necessarily embraces the wider community. *My* God is also *our* God. Believers are challenged to reject the notion of heaven as a type of spiritual individualism that reduces our interaction with others. The metaphor of heaven as a banquet suggests the presence of other invited guests. The image of the bustling new city of Jerusalem in Revelation 21 presupposes more than one occupant. Paul's understanding of the Christian community as the Body of Christ recommends itself. The unity of believers is that of a living person (organic). No one individual possesses but each person participates in a shared life (1 Cor 12:12-31). Paul implicitly challenges modern believers to look beyond their individual selves to embrace all of God's extended family. This God of Abraham, Isaac, and Jacob as well as of Sarah, Rebekah, and Rachel calls for the dismissal of all rugged individualism and the acceptance of the many-splendored community.

The Intermediate State

What about the intermediate state? According to the *Catechism of the Catholic Church*, at death the soul separates from the body that then decays. However, the soul leaves to meet God while anticipating reunion with a glorified body at the resurrection of the dead. Some authors speak of this intermediate state as "soul sleep." Others challenge the very notion of the intermediate state itself, arguing that the resurrection takes place for each individual immediately after death. (See 2 Tim 2:17, where some Christians believe that the resurrection of individuals has already occurred.)

Perhaps one would do well to consider Paul's thought on life with Christ after death but before the general resurrection. While clearly affirming the general resurrection, Paul also speaks about being with the Lord after death but without thinking in terms of an intermediate state as such. Through baptism believers already experience new life in Christ (Rom 6:4-7). (Colossians 2:12 adds that believers have been raised together with him.) In Philippians 1:23 Paul states that to die is to be with Christ. Without using the body-soul categories of Greek philosophy, he speaks in 2 Corinthians 5:6-8 about life with Christ after death. To be sure, Paul does not provide the particulars about this being with Christ that modern followers desire to know. As part of the heavenly agenda, believers should be willing to accept Paul's conviction without benefit of details, finding in the risen Jesus the source and means of activity prior to the general resurrection. Hence during this interval followers already possess the life of heaven in some measure through union with Jesus, who enjoys this life to the full in his entire risen person.

Heaven and the Ongoing Earthly Challenge

There is a tendency to regard heaven as a particular turning point after which concern for events on earth vanishes and heavenly priorities block out earthly ones. The heavenly priorities of sharing community with God and others as well as ceaseless union with Jesus take center stage while the mundane things of earthly existence are relegated to the side or completely eliminated. This myopic idea finds expression in the saying that God is in his heaven with the blessed and all is right with the world.

The biblical evidence suggests otherwise. It imposes a task and a duty for the present. The vision of the new heaven and the new earth in Revelation 21 with the glorified bodies of the blessed and the orderly structure of the new Jerusalem must move believers to initiate changes on earth. Emaciated bodies and large numbers of homeless contrast all too sharply with heavenly existence. The heaven symbol must, therefore, arouse discontentment and justified anger. The new heaven and the new earth do not endorse passivity but provoke a form of revolt against the present order. The future hope of the resurrection of the dead must break this cycle of human wretchedness. To hope for that future, one grounded in the death and resurrection of Jesus, is to challenge all those situations that continually oppress and depress the human spirit. Heaven is not a "pie in the sky, by and by" but a demanding call for radical change here and now.

Heaven and Hope

In this very fragile world many often find it difficult to trust in a new and positive future. Despair reigns supreme because the capacity to think and imagine beyond the present deplorable conditions has had no opportunity to grow and mature. Such, however, is not true of the people of Israel. They exhibit concrete confidence in and expectation for a future based on the specific promises of their God. For example, the promises to the patriarchs envision the Promised Land. As God assures Jacob, "I am with you and will protect you wherever you go, and bring you back to this land. I will never leave you until I have done what I promised you" (Gen 28:15). Because of this hope in the Promised Land, Israel throws off the shackles of Egyptian bondage and begins to head home. During the time of exile in Babylon the prophet Second Isaiah consoles his people with God's promise of a way in the wilderness and a perfectly straight highway leading home (Isa 40:3).

Hope for heaven resides in the Father's raising of Jesus from the dead and transforming him so that he conquers death once and for all. Against the bleak background of Good Friday the Father issues the ultimate challenge to hope and grounds this hope in the empty tomb on Easter

Sunday. Hope for heaven thus assumes concrete form in the resurrected person of Jesus. To the deniers of the resurrection in Corinth Paul replies, "If there is no resurrection of the dead, neither has Christ been raised" (1 Cor 15:13). Believers' hope for heaven together with the experience of the resurrection is nothing less than the risen Jesus. Such hope moves Paul to sing, "Death is swallowed up in victory" (1 Cor 15:54). Believers combine a future expectation with a present experience of God's action in Jesus. From this vantage point hope for heaven springs eternal.

Resurrection Life and Daily Struggles

The specter of "already" but "not yet" casts a long shadow over the struggles of daily life. Believers already participate in the life of the risen Jesus but have not yet attained final glory. In a sense they have a foot in each world. Daily struggles to accept only Jesus as the norm or criterion prove to be daunting, at times overwhelming. Discouragement and despair often follow in the wake of these struggles. The only apt biblical expression of this darkness is the psalm of lament: "But you, LORD, do not stay far off; / my strength, come quickly to help me. / Deliver my soul from the sword, / my life from the grip of the dog. / Save me from the lion's mouth, / my poor life from the horns of wild bulls" (Ps 22:20-22).

In 2 Corinthians Paul offers timely advice for all those who experience the temptation to give up on Jesus and pursue other models. In this letter Paul must defend his apostolic ministry. Intruders into the Corinthian community have attacked his authority and appraised him unfavorably in comparison with themselves. They have also emphasized his blatant weaknesses. In reply Paul observes that his pain and suffering actually commend him as a minister of the Gospel: "We are afflicted in every way, but not constrained; perplexed, but not driven to despair; persecuted, but not abandoned; struck down, but not destroyed; always carrying about in the body the dying of Jesus, so that the life of Jesus may also be manifested in our body" (2 Cor 4:8-10). Paradoxically, therefore, while Paul's sufferings share in the death/ dying of Jesus, they also reveal the life of the risen Jesus in him. The power of the glorified Jesus is active in all his apostolic works, particularly the painful ones. Paul firmly believes that the glory of the future resurrection in Jesus influences his present ministry so that there is power in weakness and life in death.

Another way of expressing the acceptance or rejection of Jesus as model is the conflict of wills, namely, the divine versus the human.

Daily life exposes believers to a collision of these wills so that they are tempted to prefer their own to God's. In his version of the Our Father Matthew has the following: "your will be done, on earth as in heaven" (6:10). Hence one may legitimately describe heaven as the doing of God's will. To put it another way, earth becomes heaven whenever followers opt to choose God's will over their own. In this setting Jesus once again emerges as the norm or criterion. In Gethsemane he asks his Father to let the cup pass from him. Yet he quickly qualifies his request: "yet, not as I will, but as you will" (Matt 26:39). In following this intrepid example, disciples participate in the dying and rising of Jesus with the result that heaven begins now.

Baptism and Eucharist

In Romans 6 Paul writes, "we who were baptized into Christ Jesus were baptized into his death . . . So that, just as Christ was raised from the dead by the glory of the Father, we too might live in newness of life" (6:3-4). According to Paul, believers, having been sacramentally joined with Christ in his death, are now capable of living a new life, one corresponding to the life of the risen Jesus. Paul further remarks that disciples who have thus died with Jesus will likewise live with him (6:8). The heavenly agenda must address the central role of this sacrament. It suggests that the selection list of "suitable" godparents and the venue of the postbaptismal celebration must occupy a place on the back burner. First and foremost, parents in particular must create an atmosphere in which the participation of the baptized in the death of Jesus can grow and develop. In effect, they must enable the baptized to realize his or her future destiny in the full life of the risen Jesus. Hence the " already" of baptism, while recognizing the "not yet" of complete union with Jesus in the final resurrection, must pursue a plan or program of daily living whereby that final encounter impinges on earthly existence. To be baptized with Jesus into his death is to look forward to full union with him in his resurrection.

Eucharist also requires a significant role in the heavenly agenda. The question constantly perplexing believers is how to get in touch with Jesus. Eucharist responds to this nagging question with its assurance that Jesus personally communicates himself to believers. By taking part in the Eucharist, they share in his one redeeming act, namely, his self-giving on Calvary that culminates in the glory of the resurrection. Eucharist also powerfully reminds disciples that, while they already enjoy life with Jesus, they have not yet reached their total share in that life.

Certainly Christ has died and Christ is risen. And while he will come again, followers must nourish the hope of this encounter by being nourished by the Eucharist. Eucharist and heaven go hand in hand. The bodies that partake of the Eucharist are the bodies that Jesus will ultimately transform and configure to his own body. As the Gospel of John expresses it, "Whoever eats my flesh and drinks my blood has eternal life, and I will raise him on the last day" (6:54).

Heaven and the Sabbath

In Hebrews 3–4 the author employs the image of "rest" no fewer than nine times, implying thereby its significance. Though his addressees enjoy that rest (4:3), they have not fully entered into it (4:9-10). However, they are invited to join God in the celebration of the seventh day as they continue their arduous journey of faith toward the heavenly sanctuary. There they will completely own the peace and contentment of Sabbath rest.

In Genesis 2:2-3 the biblical author introduces the Sabbath, not as a day of worship, but as a day of rest. The Israelites celebrate their trust in God who does not pass the final day in feverish activities but in peace and quiet. By entering into the rhythm of creation, they contribute to the sanctification of time. There is a time to work and a time to cease (the literal meaning of Sabbath) from work. It is a time to acknowledge God as the giver of gifts. Exodus 31:17 adds that on the seventh day God not only rests but is also refreshed.

Celebration of the Sabbath is designed to be a foretaste and foreshadowing of heaven and the end time. It anticipates to some degree the eternal rest that Jesus now offers. The Sabbath challenges believers to transform their understanding of time and seek release from its incessant demands and tyranny. It calls upon them to perceive the Sabbath as a gift and an opportunity for entrance into joyful communion with all creation, all humanity, and the Creator. In the other direction Sabbath imposes the task of reaffirming that God remains Lord over all time. Hence nonsabbatical work time and sabbatical rest time both serve the same goal, namely, to honor the Creator and heed his call to rest finally and completely in heaven. "Rest in peace" captures the meaning of both Sabbath observance and the final destiny of believers.

Heaven and the Environment

The new heaven and the new earth of Revelation 21 may give the false impression that followers can flee the scene and abdicate their responsibility to care and provide for the natural world. Biblical tradition, however, suggests otherwise. In the two creation accounts of Genesis 1–3 God designates humans as the caretakers of the created world. For example, in Genesis 1:28-30 the author introduces humans as royal figures entrusted with the awesome task of maintaining a truly human world of balance and harmony. It is hardly surprising that infidelity to God interacts with harmful effects on this world. Because of lack of faithfulness and loyalty on the part of Israel, "the land dries up, / and everything that dwells in it languishes: / The beasts of the field, / the birds of the air, / and even the fish of the sea perish" (Hos 4:3). Human sinfulness and alienation from the environment are intimately connected.

In Romans 8:18-25 Paul discusses the transformation of the entire created world. While Adam was subject to death and alienated from the natural world because of the fall, with Jesus' death and resurrection a new creation appears through the life-giving Spirit of God. Owing to this action there is the hope that creation can be freed from slavery to corruption and participate in the glorious freedom of the children of God (8:21). However, believers are challenged to see this transformation as an uncompromising ecological imperative here and now. Since resurrection life has already begun, believers must respond to this task at the present moment. Hence heaven touches earth once again. Believers will share in the new heaven and the new earth to the degree that they work now for the divinely designed relationship between humankind and the environment. The end time and the present time are partners in this demanding enterprise.

Conclusion

This heavenly agenda underlines the bond between God and humanity. Many authors have attempted to express this relentless drive to enjoy the experience of community with God. When all is said and done, perhaps Saint Augustine said it best when he wrote the following at the beginning of his *Confessions*: "You have made us for yourself, O Lord, and our heart is restless until it rests in you."

Further Readings

Avery-Peck, Alan J., and Jacob Neusner, eds. *Judaism in Late Antiquity, Part 4: Death, Life-after-Death, Resurrection and the World-to-Come in the Judaisms of Antiquity*. Leiden: Brill, 2000.

Bailey, Lloyd R., Sr. *Biblical Perspectives on Death*. Overtures to Biblical Theology. Philadelphia: Fortress, 1979.

Bauckham, Richard A. *The Fate of the Dead: Studies on the Jewish and Christian Apocalypses*. Leiden: Brill, 1998.

Benoit, Pierre, and Roland E. Murphy, eds. *Immortality and Resurrection*. Concilium. New York: Herder & Herder, 1970.

Bieringer, Reimund, Veronica Koperski, and Bianca Lataire, eds. *Resurrection in the New Testament. Festschrift J. Lambrecht*. Leuven: Leuven University/Peeters, 2002.

Charlesworth, James H., ed. *Resurrection: The Origin and Future of a Biblical Doctrine*. New York: T & T Clark, 2006.

Clark-Soles, Jaime. *Death and the Afterlife in the New Testament*. New York: T & T Clark, 2006.

Collins, John J. "Apocalyptic Eschatology as the Transcendence of Death." *Catholic Biblical Quarterly* 36 (1974): 21–43.

———. "Resurrection and Eternal Life." In *Apocalypticism and the Dead Sea Scrolls*, 110–29. New York: Routledge, 1997.

———. "Wisdom and Immortality." In *Jewish Wisdom in the Hellenistic Age*, 178–95. Louisville: Westminster John Knox, 1997.

Durrwell, Francis X. *The Resurrection: A Biblical Study*. New York: Sheed & Ward, 1960.

Fitzmyer, Joseph A. "Glory Reflected on the Face of Christ (2 Cor 3:7–4:6) and a Jewish Palestinian Motif." *Theological Studies* 42 (1981): 630–44.

———. "'To Know Him and the Power of His Resurrection.'" In *To Advance the Gospel*, 202–17. 2nd ed. Grand Rapids: Eerdmans, 1988.

Greenspoon, Leonard J. "The Origin of the Idea of Resurrection." In *Traditions in Transformation: Turning Points in Biblical Faith*, edited by Baruch Halpern and Jon D. Levenson, 247–321. Winona Lake, IN: Eisenbrauns, 1981.

Johnston, Philip. *Shades of Sheol: Death and Afterlife in the Old Testament*. Downers Grove, IL: InterVarsity, 2002.

Kaiser, Otto, and Eduard Lohse. *Death and Life*. Biblical Encounter Series. Nashville: Abingdon, 1981.

Lang, Bernhard. "Afterlife: Ancient Israel's Changing View of the World Beyond." *Bible Review* 4, no. 1 (Fall 1988): 13–23.

Madigan, Kevin J., and Jon D. Levenson. *Resurrection: The Power of God for Christians and Jews*. New Haven: Yale University, 2008.

Martin-Achard, Robert. *From Death to Life: A Study of the Development of the Doctrine of the Resurrection in the Old Testament*. Edinburgh: Oliver & Boyd, 1960.

Matera, Frank J. *New Testament Theology: Exploring Diversity and Unity*. Louisville: Westminster John Knox, 2007.

Nickelsburg, George W. E., Jr. *Resurrection, Immortality, and Eternal Life in Intertestamental Judaism*. Harvard Theological Studies. Cambridge: Harvard University, 1972.

Perkins, Pheme. *Resurrection: New Testament Witness and Contemporary Reflection*. Garden City, NY: Doubleday, 1984.

Roetzel, Calvin J. "'As Dying and Behold We Live': Death and Resurrection in Paul's Theology." *Interpretation* 46 (1992): 5–18.

Schneiders, Sandra M. "The Resurrection (of the Body) in the Fourth Gospel: A Key to Johannine Spirituality." In *Life in Abundance: Studies of John's Gospel in Tribute to Raymond E. Brown*, edited by John R. Donahue, 168–98. Collegeville, MN: Liturgical Press, 2005.

Stanley, David M. *Christ's Resurrection in Pauline Soteriology*. Analecta Biblica. Rome: Biblical Institute, 1961.

Sutcliffe, Edmund F. *The Old Testament and the Future Life*. 2nd ed. Westminster: Newman, 1947.

Talbert, Charles H. "The Place of the Resurrection in the Theology of Luke." *Interpretation* 46 (1992): 19–30.

Tromp, Nicholas J. *Primitive Conceptions of Death and the Netherworld in the Old Testament*. Biblica et Orientalia. Rome: Biblical Institute, 1969.

Van Iersel, Bas, and Edward Schillebeeckx, eds. *Heaven*. Concilium. New York: Seabury, 1979.

Vawter, Bruce. "Intimations of Immortality and the Old Testament." *Journal of Biblical Literature* 91 (1972): 158–71.

Wright, N. Thomas. *The Resurrection of the Son of God*. Minneapolis: Fortress, 2003.